MW01126312

Amazing
Fishing
Facts and Trivia

Amazing
Fishing
Facts and Trivia

by
Tony Lolli

CHARTWELL
BOOKS, INC.

A QUARTO BOOK

Published in 2012 by
Chartwell Books, Inc.
A division of Book Sales, Inc.
276 Fifth Avenue Suite 206
New York, New York 10001
USA

Copyright © 2012 Quarto Inc.

ISBN: 978-0-7858-2900-3

Conceived, designed,
and produced by
Quarto Publishing plc
The Old Brewery
6 Blundell Street
London N7 9BH

QUA: AFFF

Editor & designer:
Michelle Pickering
Art director: Caroline Guest
Proofreader: Claire Waite Brown
Indexer: Dorothy Frame

Creative director: Moira Clinch
Publisher: Paul Carslake

Color separation by Modern Age
Repro House Ltd, Hong Kong
Printed by Midas Printing
International Ltd, China

Contents

The contents of this book are completely random, so
that each time you open the book, you will discover an
amazing variety of facts and trivia about the world of fish
and fishing. If you wish to locate a particular category of
information, however, this contents listing is organized
into topics. There is also an index at the end of the book.

FISHING TACKLE

LURES

BAITS

FRESHWATER SPECIES

TERMINOLOGY & PHRASES

MISCELLANEOUS

INTRODUCTION

A fisherman has been described as a jerk at one end of a line waiting for a jerk at the other. Having been a "jerk" for more than 50 years, I can assure you that fishing is the most fun you can have while standing up—or sitting down. But, I digress.

Fish and fishing have been important in culture and commerce for millennia, but only in the recent past have they become associated with recreation. Regardless of the reason, fish and fishing continue to be of interest to a wide cross-section of the inhabitants of this planet. For some, they provide a major source of protein; for others, they provide a necessary respite in the company of kindred spirits. Who's to say which is more important?

With more than 30,000 species of fish, and more being discovered each year, we'll continue to discover amazing fish facts for a long time to come. For example, the largest fish is the 59-foot (18-meter) whale shark, and the smallest, *Photocorynus spiniceps*, measures a miniscule 0.24 inches (6.2 mm). The fastest fish is the sailfish, traveling at 68 miles per hour (109 kph), while the seahorse can only manage a sedate 0.001 miles per hour. Quite a range of performances—no?

Methods of collecting fish vary from the ridiculous, such as shooting pike, to the sublime—tickling trout and lifting them out of the water when they go into a trance. Methods such as fly fishing have been in existence for 2,000 years, while others are more recent—angling for toothy garfish only became possible with the advent of woven nylon rope in the 20th century. There's a fishing technique for everyone's taste—kings, presidents, and Average Jills. Some are used by anglers around the world, while others are little known except to a small group of reprobates and ne'er-do-wells who keep the practices alive.

There are as many opportunities for angling as there are motives—you can choose to angle as a means of contemplating your place in the natural order of the universe, or your ultimate goal may be to compete as a member of your country's international fishing team. Wherever your particular interest in fish and fishing lies, there's plenty in this book to keep you entertained for hours. Read on!

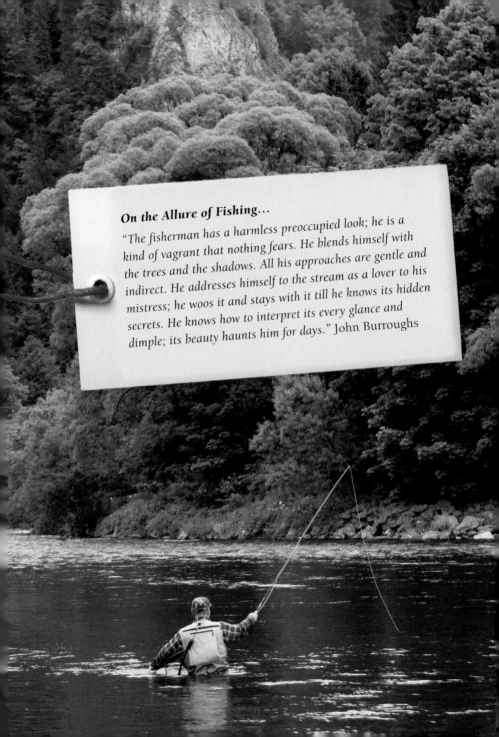

On the Allure of Fishing…

"The fisherman has a harmless preoccupied look; he is a kind of vagrant that nothing fears. He blends himself with the trees and the shadows. All his approaches are gentle and indirect. He addresses himself to the stream as a lover to his mistress; he woos it and stays with it till he knows its hidden secrets. He knows how to interpret its every glance and dimple; its beauty haunts him for days." John Burroughs

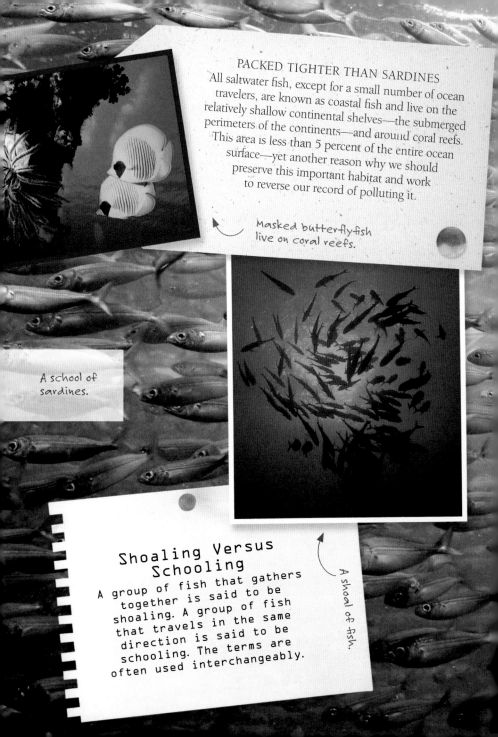

PACKED TIGHTER THAN SARDINES

All saltwater fish, except for a small number of ocean travelers, are known as coastal fish and live on the relatively shallow continental shelves—the submerged perimeters of the continents—and around coral reefs. This area is less than 5 percent of the entire ocean surface—yet another reason why we should preserve this important habitat and work to reverse our record of polluting it.

Masked butterflyfish live on coral reefs.

A school of sardines.

Shoaling Versus Schooling

A group of fish that gathers together is said to be shoaling. A group of fish that travels in the same direction is said to be schooling. The terms are often used interchangeably.

A shoal of fish.

Hooked on History

✦ It is believed that the earliest hooks were probably made by Cro-Magnon people living 35,000 to 10,000 years ago, using a short segment of branched hawthorn. Wooden hooks made from hawthorn were used by fishermen from Wales and Sweden until recent times.

✦ Other hook material included carved bone and antler. Bone hooks, 7,000 to 8,000 years old, have been found in Norway.

✦ Copper hooks from Mesopotamia are believed to be 1,800 years old. Similar hooks have been found in Italy and Egypt.

✦ Iron and steel hooks began appearing in the 1600s. Many were made by craftsmen who could make steel from bog iron.

Oldest Hooks

The oldest fishhooks that have been found to date are made of bone and were found in what was Czechoslovakia. They are estimated to be 20,000 years old. There is no written record to explain how they were baited or cast. However, thousands of years later, around the 8th century B.C.E., the ancient Greek poet Homer is credited with writing:

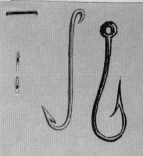

"Casting into the deep the horn of an ox, and as he catches each [fish] flings it up writhing."

← Homer

FISHY QUOTES

✦ *"Let your hook be always cast. In the pool where you least expect it, will be fish."* Ovid

✦ *"Beauty without grace is the hook without the bait."* Ralph Waldo Emerson

✦ *"When you bait your hook with your heart, the fish always bite."* John Burroughs

✦ *"A fishing rod is a stick with a hook at one end and a fool at the other."* Samuel Johnson

BARRACUDA

+ Barracuda are aggressive fish with a mouth full of impressive teeth. Long, thin predators, they are fast enough to chase down prey fish. Thanks to their effective dentition, they can feed on prey larger than themselves by tearing out and eating pieces of flesh.

+ The barracuda strikes at any flashing object that it mistakes for prey. These fish have been known to bite people who were wading, swimming, or diving. Although attacking people is not common, their exceptional teeth cause considerable damage.

+ Barracuda prefer warm tropical waters. They are prized by anglers for their speed and strength. The IGFA world record for the great barracuda is 85 pounds (38.55 kg).

+ Should a barracuda be caught and prepared for the table, it can get its revenge because many barracuda are poisonous.

Fish, poissons, pesci, pescados, fische, vissen, peixes...

BABEL FISH

Not one but three definitions exist for the babel fish. Take your pick:

❶ From Douglas Adams's book *The Hitchhiker's Guide to the Galaxy* (1979), a fictitious fish that performs instant translations.

❷ A Norwegian musical group named for Adams's creature.

❸ A Yahoo! application for translations, named for Adams's creature.

A group of barracuda is called a battery. One is enough.

FISHY QUOTES

✦ *"There is certainly something in angling that tends to produce a gentleness of spirit and a pure serenity of mind."*
Washington Irving

✦ *"Many men go fishing all of their lives without knowing it is not fish they are after."*
Henry David Thoreau

✦ *"The angler forgets most of the fish he catches, but he does not forget the streams and lakes in which they were caught."*
Charles K. Fox

✦ *"Fishing is not so much getting fish as it is a state of mind, a lure for the human soul into refreshment."*
Herbert Hoover

✦ *"For the true angler, fishing produces a deep, unspoken joy, born of longing for that which is quiet and peaceful, and fostered by an inbred love of communing with nature."* Thaddeus Norris

✦ *"The angling fever is a very real disease and can only be cured by the application of cold water and fresh, untainted air."*
Theodore Gordon

Solunar Tables: Predicting the Unpredictable?

Solunar tables—one of the longest running, non-comic-strip features, first published in 1936—provide guidance about the best times to fish. Their creator, John Alden Knight, compiled a list of 33 factors that might affect fishing success. After examining each factor, he reduced the list to three—sun (sol), moon (lunar), and tide. He discovered that, in addition to the major periods, there were intermediate times pointing toward increased fish activity. With the assistance of the United States Naval Observatory and GPS technology, Knight's tables have now become even more precise.

GO FISH: THE CARD GAME

In this favorite card game of children, each player, in turn, asks the player to the left if he or she has any specific card—for example, "Have any eights?" The player asked must give up his or her eights. If the player asked does not have any eights, he or she says, 'Go fish," and the asker takes a card from the deck. The first to collect and lay down all four of every card in his or her hand wins.

Ancient Egyptian fishing and hunting scene.

Ancient Records

Angling appears to have been invented in several places at different times.

✦ The ancient Egyptians provided the earliest account of angling, but in art rather than in writing. An Egyptian angling scene from about 2000 B.C.E. shows figures fishing with rod and line and with nets.

✦ A 4th-century B.C.E. Chinese written account refers to fishing with a silk line, a hook made from a needle, and a bamboo rod.

✦ References to fishing are also found in ancient Greek, Assyrian, Roman, and Jewish writings. All this suggests that fishing has always been fundamental for sustaining societies across the world.

FISHY QUOTES

✦ *"Give me a fish and I eat for a day. Teach me to fish and I eat for a lifetime."* Chinese proverb

✦ *"Give a man a fish and he eats for a day. Teach him to fish and he sits in a boat all day drinking beer."* Anon.

✦ *"Sell a man a fish, he eats for a day, teach a man how to fish, you ruin a wonderful business opportunity."* Karl Marx

FISH NAMED FOR OTHER CREATURES

Some similarities may be in the eye
of the beholder, but some names seem
to be stretching our credulity to
the extreme.

- Alligator gar
- Bull trout
- Bullhead
- Catfish
- Dogfish
- Dolphin-fish
- Goatfish
- Hogfish
- Leopard shark
- Lionfish
- Lizardfish
- Parrotfish
- Peacock cichlid
- Peacock hind
- Porcupinefish
- Porkfish
- Ratfish
- Redhorse
- Roosterfish
- Scorpionfish
- Sea raven
- Sea robin
- Shark minnow
- Sheepshead
- Snakehead
- Squirrelfish
- Tiger shark
- Toadfish
- Wolffish

VENOMOUS FISH

Avoid licking fish that produce venom, such as stonefish, stargazers, lionfish, and scorpionfish. Licking a toadfish is also hazardous, but may result in the appearance of a princess.

Lionfish

STONEFISH

The stonefish holds the distinction of being the earth's ugliest fish. Patient hunters, they lie still on the ocean floor in tropical waters and wait, sometimes for days, for their prey to swim by. Stonefish also have poisonous barbs covering their back. Each year, several humans are killed by stepping on this fish.

NATURAL BAITS: MAGGOTS AND OTHER LARVAE

The larvae and pupae of a huge number of insects are probably the most common type of natural bait used by anglers.

✤ **Casters:** The pupae of large maggots, widely used as bait for most species of fish, are known as casters. When exposed to the air, they become crisp, and will remain best on a hook.

✤ **Disco maggots:** This term denotes fluorescent-colored maggots. Anglers are attracted to them. Sometimes the fish also like them.

✤ **Gozzers:** These homebred maggots are much preferred by bream. While not commercially available, bluebottle fly larvae can be bred on fresh meat kept in the dark. This technique is not for the faint of heart.

✤ **Jokers:** These are gnat larvae. This tiny red bait is a favorite of match anglers for small fish on canals.

✤ **Mealworms:** These are the larval form of the mealworm beetle and are especially effective for catching roach.

✤ **Pinkies:** These are small, off-white maggots. These larvae of the greenbottle fly are lively and preferred by canal match

Dyed maggots

anglers. Common dyed colors include red, bronze, and pink.

✤ **Squatts:** These are yet another type of maggot. These small, white maggots are the larval form of houseflies and can be used as groundbait or impaled on tiny hooks when fishing for small fish.

✤ **Joker powder:** This is used to separate gnat larvae (jokers), making for a more even distribution into groundbaits.

✤ **Maggot binder:** This powder is used to hold maggots in a ball shape so that it can be catapulted without flying off in many directions. Powdered maggot balls can be delivered more accurately than loose maggots.

✤ **Scalding maggots:** Scalding maggots in boiling water kills them so that they cannot crawl into the bottom silt when broadcast into a fishing area.

The Eyes Have It

Fish do not have eyelids. Blinking in mammals cleans and
wets the eyes. Water provides both functions for fish. Without
eyelids, fish use other methods to protect themselves from eye
damage due to bright sunshine. They find a shaded spot or
greater depth. The only exception is the shark. It has a
nictitating membrane that covers the shark's eye when
it is engaged in violent, active feeding.

Mealworm—
a favorite
snack of
the roach.

The roach is
also known as the
redeye because of its
distinctive eye color.

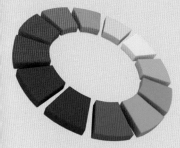

Do Fish See Colors?

Some do; some don't. It all depends on where the fish
live. Shallow-water fish see colors especially well. Their
eyes have an abundance of cones, the color-sensing
organs. Those fish living at the bottom of the ocean do
not see colors because there is so little light. Instead,
they have an abundance of rods to facilitate vision
in low light conditions. It all works out in the end.

EVOLUTION OF THE FISHING ROD

Over time, many materials have been used for creating fishing rods. The essential characteristic is the ability to recover from bending. The list of materials includes:

A basic fishing rod constructed from a single length of bamboo.

✴ **Wood:** The earliest rods were nothing more than lengths of saplings up to 20 feet (6 meters) long. A line of equal length was tied to the tip of the sapling, and swinging the rod delivered the bait, lure, or fly. In the early 1870s, lancewood, hickory, and greenheart were valued for rods because of their flexibility and strength.

✴ **Bamboo:** Bamboo was also popular. The first bamboo rod maker is in dispute, but split bamboo rods showed up in the mid-1800s.

✴ **Steel:** In the early 1900s, steel rods were manufactured at a much lower cost than handcrafted bamboo rods. Telescopic steel rods were popular for a time.

✴ **Fiberglass:** Following World War II, fishing rods made of fiberglass, a man-made fiber, were developed. Since that time, other fibers such as graphite, boron, carbon fiber, and titanium have found their way into fishing rods.

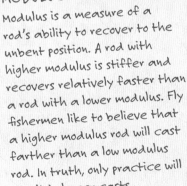

MODULUS

Modulus is a measure of a rod's ability to recover to the unbent position. A rod with higher modulus is stiffer and recovers relatively faster than a rod with a lower modulus. Fly fishermen like to believe that a higher modulus rod will cast farther than a low modulus rod. In truth, only practice will result in longer casts.

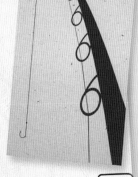

The bull shark migrates between fresh and salt water.

TARPON: HEAVYWEIGHT LEAPER

Tarpon are an angler's delight because, when hooked, they can leap 10 feet (3 meters) out of the water. The IGFA world record is 286 pounds 9 ounces (129.98 kg). These large silver fish often remain hooked up for only a few seconds. Anglers prefer sardines, anchovies, and mullet for live bait. Fly fishermen usually cast specific tarpon patterns that resemble nothing in nature.

Get Out of Town

There is more than one type of fish migration, and not all involve spawning.

* **Potamodromous:** Migration is limited to fresh water only. Most trout migrate upstream to find appropriate bottom gravel to build a nest for spawning, and then migrate back downstream where food is more plentiful.

* **Oceanodromous:** Migration takes place only in salt water. Species such as sharks and tarpon gather together for spawning in the open ocean.

* **Diadromous:** This refers to fish that travel between both fresh and salt water. Arctic char and the three-spined stickleback are examples. There are three subcategories of diadromous migrations:
  A) Anadromous: Ocean fish, such as salmon and striped bass, enter fresh water specifically for spawning.
  B) Catadromous: Freshwater fish, such as eels, travel to the ocean to spawn.
  C) Amphidromous: Fish such as the bull shark of Lake Nicaragua and the Zambezi River migrate to and from the ocean but not to breed.

Wading Staff

A wading staff is not an aquatic maître d'. It is a stick-like device that is used as a third leg to keep wading anglers from falling into the water—something they do with alarming regularity when failing to use a wading staff. Some wading staffs are collapsible and ride in a holster on the angler's belt. Of course, getting the staff out and assembled while in the act of falling is not to be attempted by anyone with normal reflexes. Cautious and dry anglers deploy their staffs at the first sign of dangerous conditions.

Menhaden

Fish Fertilizer

* Fish, like menhaden, are the basis for fish fertilizer. After being cooked at 212°F (100°C), a press separates the oil from the solids. The solids can then be processed into animal feeds or fertilizer.

* Although children in the United States are taught that Squanto, a Native American, first taught early colonialists to use fish as fertilizer, the practice was known to ancient Egyptians and pre-Columbian agrarians.

FISHY QUOTES

✦ *"The more you fish the more you start seeing things the way a farmer does: It doesn't have to be great, just please don't let it be awful."* John Gierach

✦ *"A fisherman has many dreams. Sometimes dreams, even those of a fisherman, come true."* Zane Grey

✦ *"Fishing is a perfectible art, in which, never the less, no man is ever perfect."* Gifford Pinchot

✦ *"There is no use in walking five miles to fish when you can depend on being just as unsuccessful here at home."* Mark Twain

✦ *"Fishing seems to be divided, like sex, into three most unequal parts, the two larger, by far, are anticipation and recollection, and in between, by far the smallest of the three, actual performance."* Arnold Gingrich

✦ *"There is no substitute for fishing sense, and if a man doesn't have it, verily, he may cast like an angel and still use his creel largely to transport sandwiches and beer."* Robert Traver

Vested Interests

+ Fly fishermen insist on carrying more equipment than is necessary. That is why you can always hear them coming, as the clanging tonnage in their vest signals their arrival.

+ Fly-fishing pioneer Lee Wulff is credited with inventing the fishing vest. He realized that contemporary fly fishermen were carrying so much tackle that they required some kind of multi-pocketed clothing to accommodate their holdings. Wulff started with a wool shirt, cut off the sleeves, made additional pockets from the sleeve material, and sewed the pockets onto the shirt's front.

+ Wulff's garment caught on and every fly fisherman worthy of the title now wears this iconic garb. Wulff remained active as a fly-fishing luminary until his death in 1991 at age 86, when his plane crashed as he was renewing his private pilot's license.

A fly fisherman wearing a vest, each pocket filled to capacity.

Vest Equipment

Here are some of the things that the well-turned-out angler carries in his or her vest.

❖ Camera	❖ Hook hone	❖ Strike indicators
❖ Clippers/Nippers	❖ Knife	❖ Tape measure
❖ Emergency light	❖ Knot-tying tool	❖ Thermometer
❖ Flashlight	❖ Leader straightener	❖ Tippet spool holder
❖ Flask	❖ Leader wallet	❖ Tippet wheels
❖ Fly boxes	❖ Leaders	❖ Wading staff
❖ Fly floatant	❖ Magnifier	❖ Weighing scale
❖ Fly-line cleaner	❖ Micro split shot	❖ Zingers
❖ Fly sink	❖ Net	
❖ Fly threader	❖ Personal flotation device	
❖ Forceps	❖ Polarized sunglasses	
❖ Headlamp	❖ Scissors	

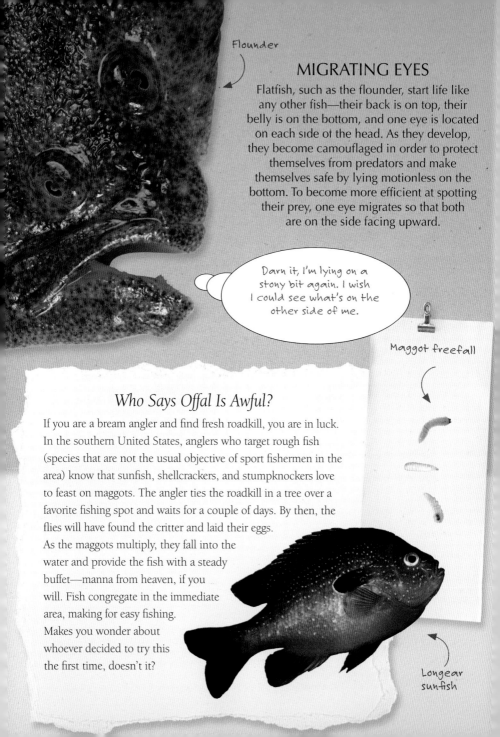

Flounder

MIGRATING EYES

Flatfish, such as the flounder, start life like any other fish—their back is on top, their belly is on the bottom, and one eye is located on each side of the head. As they develop, they become camouflaged in order to protect themselves from predators and make themselves safe by lying motionless on the bottom. To become more efficient at spotting their prey, one eye migrates so that both are on the side facing upward.

Darn it, I'm lying on a stony bit again. I wish I could see what's on the other side of me.

Maggot freefall

Who Says Offal Is Awful?

If you are a bream angler and find fresh roadkill, you are in luck. In the southern United States, anglers who target rough fish (species that are not the usual objective of sport fishermen in the area) know that sunfish, shellcrackers, and stumpknockers love to feast on maggots. The angler ties the roadkill in a tree over a favorite fishing spot and waits for a couple of days. By then, the flies will have found the critter and laid their eggs. As the maggots multiply, they fall into the water and provide the fish with a steady buffet—manna from heaven, if you will. Fish congregate in the immediate area, making for easy fishing. Makes you wonder about whoever decided to try this the first time, doesn't it?

Longear sun-fish

Flounder

+ **Winter flounder:** So named because it spends the winter in shallow inshore water, this flatfish has one of the shortest migrations. It seldom leaves estuaries and coastal areas. Spawning in January through March, smaller three-year-old females lay 500,000 eggs, while larger 8-pounders (3.6 kg) lay 1,500,000 eggs. It was recently discovered that flounder may return to the same site to spawn year after year. Unlike other flatfish, the winter flounder's eggs do not float but instead sink to the bottom, where they hatch after 15 to 18 days.

+ **Summer flounder:** Also known as fluke, this flatfish is much sought after for its flavor. On average, adults weigh 2 to 5 pounds (0.9 to 2.3 kg), but the record is over 20 pounds (9 kg). Smaller females lay 460,000 eggs, while larger ones lay 4,200,000 eggs. Unlike the lazy winter flounder, the summer flounder relies on its eyesight to find prey, and it often leaps out of the water when chasing schools of baitfish.

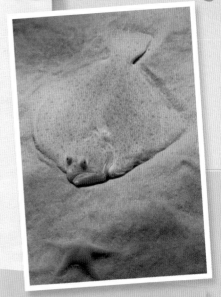

When frightened, flounder quickly bury themselves in the sand, with only their eyes unburied.

The hagfish predates dinosaurs and lives in the ocean depths.

FISH RESEARCH

Ichthyology is the study of fish. Zoologists who study fish are called ichthyologists. The three groups of fish studied by ichthyologists include bony fish (almost any you may care to name), cartilaginous fish (such as sharks), and jawless fish. Jawless!?! Yes, lampreys and the hagfish.

Flounder Tramping

Although it may sound fictitious, flounder tramping has been used in the estuaries of southwest Scotland for centuries. It is practiced by wading in shallow water and standing on the flounder (or other flatfish) before spearing the fish. Question: With kilts or sans kilts?

Black Bass:
The Three Subspecies

Smallmouth bass

❶ **Largemouth bass:** This species has a large upper jaw that extends behind the eye. Their colors range from green to black. They prefer shallower, slower, warmer water. Reed beds are often preferred spawning areas, because they are shallow and the bottom is easily cleared during nest-building.

❷ **Smallmouth bass:** This species looks different from the others because it is more bronze or brown and has side markings that look like stripes. It has a smaller mouth than the largemouth, and the upper jaw does not extend beyond its eye. The eye may have red color in it. The smallmouth prefers deeper, cooler, cleaner water, and 90 percent of smallmouth are found in water deeper than 15 feet (4.6 meters). It is more likely to be found in rocky cover. In streams, it prefers current. Smallmouth orient toward boulders, rock beds, tree trunks, and bridge abutments, but they are not found in weed beds.

❸ **Spotted bass:** Divide the characteristics and preferences of largemouth and smallmouth bass and you will have spotted bass preferences. Spotted bass are also known as Kentucky bass. They are not as large as smallmouth, and do not have the stripes of smallmouth. They school more often than either of the other species, and locate around deep, rocky structure.

Spotted bass

A largemouth bass chasing a spinnerbait lure.

LARGEMOUTH BASS VIRUS: A RELATIVELY RECENT VILLAIN

First discovered in Florida in 1991, largemouth bass virus (LMBV) now shows up in the whole southern United States. It affects the swim bladder of largemouth bass, smallmouth bass, spotted bass, Suwanee bass, bluegill, redbreasted sunfish, white crappie, and black crappie. However, it seems to cause death only in largemouth bass. Infected fish will be near the surface, have trouble staying upright, and have difficulty swimming. LMBV can be transmitted through the water, by fish-to-fish contact, and by consuming infected prey. Because LMBV can survive in the water for up to seven days, it can be transferred in the live wells of boats. LMBV cannot be eradicated in the wild.

Phish Phobias

The Greek word "ichthys" means fish. Ichthyophobia is a fear of fish and may include fear of eating fish. Fear of being eaten by fish, specifically sharks (no kidding), is a subtype known as galeophobia. The Greek word "galeos" means small shark.

Bait-casting reel

BAIT CASTING

Little is known of the origin of bait casting. However, in 1651, in British literature, there was mention of a "wind" (i.e. winding mechanism) mounted on a rod. An earlier Chinese pictorial reference from 1195 shows a wind in use. Until the 1800s, the reel was used only to store line. Next, multiplying reels, capable of retrieving more line with each turn of the handle, were produced by jewelers who had experience with intricate mechanisms. Once mass production lowered the price, the sport of bait fishing was embraced by a larger group of anglers. Bait-casting reels have spools that sit at a right angle to the rod. When a cast is made, the reel turns as the line goes out.

GEAR RATIO

This is not a measure of the number of items allowed by each angler. Instead, it is a measure of how many revolutions a reel makes for every turn of the handle. A higher gear ratio brings in more line per turn than does a reel with a lower ratio. Species requiring fast retrieves are more efficiently fished with high gear ratio reels.

Rock Bass

Thousands of children have learned to fish by catching rock bass. This member of the sunfish family strikes any bait readily. It is also known by many other names, including goggle-eye perch, rock sunfish, black perch, and redeye. In addition, the flesh of rock bass is light and mild. The main identifying characteristic of the rock bass is its very large red to orange-red eyes—ergo, its nicknames.

Rock bass

Stages of Fish Development: A Matter of Perspective

According to anglers, the stages of fish development are:

1) "That's a nice fish."
2) "Get the net."
3) "Get the camera."

Scientists, however, having less imagination, identify the stages as:

1) Egg
2) Yolk fry (hatchlings with the egg yolk sac still attached)
3) Fry (from the first feeding after the yolk sac is used up)
4) Fingerling (about the size of an adult index finger)
5) Yearling (a year old)
6) Adult

FISHY QUOTES

✦ "Fish and visitors smell after three days." Benjamin Franklin

✦ "Fishing consists of a series of misadventures interspersed by occasional moments of glory." Howard Marshall

✦ "Some men would rather be photographed with their fish than with their wives." Gwen Cooper

✦ "Men and fish are alike. They both get into trouble when they open their mouths." Anon.

✦ "Like 'military intelligence' and 'airline cuisine,' 'sophisticated angler' is an oxymoron." Thomas McGuane

GORGING AND DISGORGING

One of humankind's earliest tools was the gorge—a short piece of wood or bone, pointed at both ends, that was tied slightly off-center to a fishing line. When baited, the fish would swallow the gorge. The fisherman pulled on the line to lodge the gorge in the fish's throat and then pulled in the fish. When a fish threw the gorge, it was said to have disgorged. A specific tool, still in use today, for freeing a deeply hooked fish is known as a disgorger.

Disgorger

SALMON LIFE CYCLE

The life cycle of the different salmon species is similar, with the main difference being that Pacific salmon die after spawning, whereas Atlantic salmon may spawn more than once. Landlocked salmon do not migrate.

❋ **Spawning:** In the fall, salmon leave the ocean and swim upstream until they reach the same small tributary where they were born. Females use their tail to "sweep" a nest (known as a redd) in the gravel. As she deposits her eggs, males fertilize them. Next, the female sweeps gravel over the fertilized eggs and they remain below the gravel until they hatch out.

❋ **Hatchlings:** The hatchlings, called alevins, feed on the egg yolk sac for six weeks. Next, they swim up through the gravel and are called parr. They remain in the river for two to five years before they migrate downstream to the ocean.

❋ **Juveniles:** As they reach the ocean, their coloration changes from trout-like to silver and they are called smolt. Schools of smolt migrate near Greenland and share feeding grounds with salmon from North America and Europe. Smolt that migrate back to their rivers after only two years weigh 2 to 4 pounds (0.9 to 1.8 kg).

❋ **Adults:** Mature salmon returning to spawn weigh between 10 and 100 pounds (4.5 and 45 kg), depending on the species.

Hatchling with yolk sac.

THE VIBERT BOX

In the early 1950s, Dr. Richard Vibert, a French fisheries researcher, invented the Vibert box, a fish incubator. Similar to a plastic cage, it is used to hold fertilized eggs so that they can be placed in man-made nests in natural rivers and streams. The box is covered with gravel, just as it would be if the spawning female were to cover her eggs. When the eggs hatch, the yolk nourishes the fry for several days.

The bars on the Vibert box are spaced so that the yolk fry cannot get out of the box until the yolk sac is absorbed. After leaving the box, the fry find their way up through the gravel and begin their life in the stream as free-swimming fish.

Spawning male sockeye salmon.

Bears fishing for salmon as the fish leap up Brooks Falls in Katmai National Park, Alaska.

Why do I never get the best fishing spot?

Jump on It

The several species of salmon have one thing in common—they are jumpers.

+ Leaping is a migration necessity because salmon leave salt water, swim up rivers, and must find the same areas where they were hatched in order to spawn. Frequently, salmon must leap in order to clear falls to get to their nursery waters.

+ Slow-motion photography reveals that the salmon do not make the entire height of the falls in one leap. They get a running start, jump, and then swim against the falling water to take them to the top of falls that are too high to jump—no wonder they need to rest frequently on their spawning journey.

+ Occasionally, large grizzly bears figure out where salmon will be leaping and position themselves where the fishing is easiest. Some bears have been photographed, mouth agape, as the salmon jump into the bear's mouth.

MOST POPULAR ANGLING SPECIES

According to the American Sportfishing Association, the most angler hours are spent in pursuit of the following species:

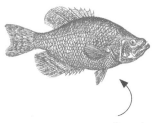

Crappie

FRESH WATER

◆ Bass
◆ Bullhead
◆ Carp
◆ Catfish
◆ Char
◆ Crappie
◆ Grayling
◆ Muskellunge
◆ Perch
◆ Pickerel
◆ Pike
◆ Salmon
◆ Shad
◆ Splake
◆ Sturgeon
◆ Sunfish
◆ Trout
◆ Walleye

SALT WATER

★ Amberjack
★ Barracuda
★ Bluefish
★ Bonefish
★ Bonito
★ Corbina
★ Dorado
★ Drum
★ Flounder
★ Grouper
★ Jack cravalle
★ Kingfish
★ Mackerel
★ Marlin
★ Pollack
★ Pompano
★ Porgy
★ Sailfish
★ Sea bass
★ Shark
★ Snook
★ Striped bass
★ Swordfish
★ Tarpon
★ Tuna
★ Wahoo
★ Weakfish
★ Yellowtail

The sailfish is prized by saltwater anglers for its energetic fight.

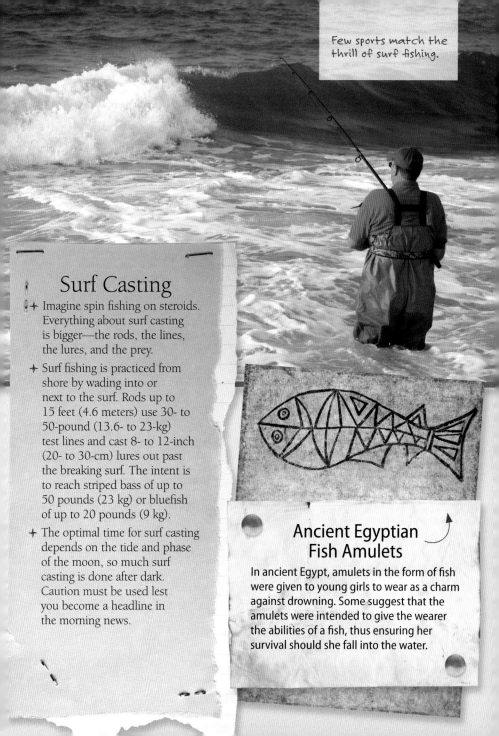

Few sports match the thrill of surf fishing.

Surf Casting

- Imagine spin fishing on steroids. Everything about surf casting is bigger—the rods, the lines, the lures, and the prey.

- Surf fishing is practiced from shore by wading into or next to the surf. Rods up to 15 feet (4.6 meters) use 30- to 50-pound (13.6- to 23-kg) test lines and cast 8- to 12-inch (20- to 30-cm) lures out past the breaking surf. The intent is to reach striped bass of up to 50 pounds (23 kg) or bluefish of up to 20 pounds (9 kg).

- The optimal time for surf casting depends on the tide and phase of the moon, so much surf casting is done after dark. Caution must be used lest you become a headline in the morning news.

Ancient Egyptian Fish Amulets

In ancient Egypt, amulets in the form of fish were given to young girls to wear as a charm against drowning. Some suggest that the amulets were intended to give the wearer the abilities of a fish, thus ensuring her survival should she fall into the water.

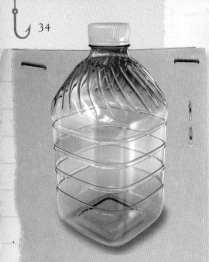

JUG FISHING

This involves tying a 5- to 6-foot (1.5- to 1.8-meter) line to a sealed jug—something like a plastic gallon (4-liter) jug or a 2-liter pop bottle. The hook is baited and the jug is allowed to float with the current. Those jugs that bob unnaturally indicate that a fish has taken the bait. The fisherman boats to the jug and recovers the fish. A large number of jugs, all out at the same time, result in fast action. Bream and catfish are commonly caught using this method.

TAKING STOCK OF STOCKING

Not all fish are naturally reproducing in all areas. Sometimes Mother Nature needs a little help, so fish raised in hatcheries or otherwise trapped are placed in other waters. A number of relocation methods are used. These include:

❋ Trucking and dumping by hose or pail.

❋ Floating a live box and distributing fish along a river.

❋ Moving large cans on horseback.

❋ Snowmobiling over frozen lakes and boring a hole through the ice.

❋ Flying tanks by helicopter and gently dropping the fish into lakes.

❋ Loading tanks onto airplanes and dropping fish as the plane makes a low, slow pass over a lake.

Dropping fish from a plane does not harm the fish but it certainly surprises them.

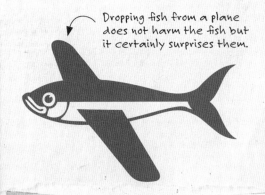

Fishing Season: An Open and Shut Case

The period of the year when fishing is allowed is known as the fishing season. It has nothing to do with the calendar, but everything to do with protecting fish from overfishing and making them safe when they are spawning.

The whale shark is the biggest fish in the sea.

SHANTY TOWN

Shanty town is the term given to a collection of ice-fishing shanties (ice houses/bob houses). In places with sufficient ice and long winters, a shanty town may remain in place for several months. The shanties are dragged onto the ice as soon as the ice is safe, and remain there until the end of the season. A feature common to all is the ability to fish through a hole in the floor. Spartan shanties are little more than a place to get out of the wind. Luxury shanties have beds, cookstove, heater, television, and every other appliance known to humankind. Well-equipped shanties have their own power generators. None of them needs a refrigerator—the beer is kept outside.

A Question of Scale

❖ **Supersize:** The largest saltwater fish is the whale shark. The largest verified specimen weighed 47,000 pounds (21,300 kg) and was $41\frac{1}{2}$ feet (12.6 meters) long, but there are reports of whale sharks up to 79,000 pounds (35,800 kg) and 59 feet (18 meters). The largest freshwater fish is the Mekong giant catfish, weighing in at 650 pounds (295 kg) and measuring 10 feet (3 meters) long.

❖ **Midget fins:** The female *Paedocypris progenetica* from Indonesia, which is transparent and has no head bones, attains the fantastic length of 0.31 inches (7.9 mm), making it the smallest freshwater fish. The male *Photocorynus spiniceps* is the smallest saltwater fish, measuring 0.24 inches (6.2 mm).

A shanty town—or ice-fishing camp—on a lake.

A fly fisherman making a cast.

WHY ALL THE HOOPLA OVER FLY FISHING?

The earliest fishing (long rod, line, and fly), as practiced over 2,000 years ago, was most like contemporary fly fishing. These origins create a sense of tradition among fly fishermen. Casting such small lures does not disturb the water, so the fly caster feels more in tune with the environment. Effective fly casting is also a practiced skill—and fly fishermen are prideful of their skills.

Fly Casting

In fly casting, the rod casts a relatively heavy line and the fly—an artificial imitation of an insect—goes along for the ride.

+ In its earliest form, fly casting used a line tied to the tip of a rod. The line was approximately the same length as the rod. No reel was used.

+ It was unencumbered by heavy lures, and the earliest lures were in fact nothing more than pieces of fabric designed to get the fish's attention and cause it to strike.

+ Years later, lures were created to imitate the size and color of natural insects, or flies, found in the area.

+ In the 1800s, fly reels were designed to hold longer lines and casting was a way to cast a line longer than the rod.

Creel (wicker basket)

Creel Limit

Whether or not you use a creel to hold your catch, many areas restrict the number of fish you may keep in any one day. This limit is known as the creel limit.

FISHY QUOTES

✦ *"Fly fishing is the most fun you can have standing up."* Arnold Gingrich

✦ *"More than half the intense enjoyment of fly fishing is derived from the beautiful surroundings, the satisfaction felt from being in the open air, the new lease of life secured thereby, and the many, many pleasant recollections of all one has seen, heard, and done."* Charles F. Orvis

✦ *"The very mechanics of fly fishing are restful and relaxing. The act of rhythmically casting one's rod and line to and fro, slows one's mood to the tempo of the gentle winds and undulating currents."* Martin J. Keane

✦ *"The literature on fly fishing is a minefield of disagreement…on all issues of momentous inconsequence."* Brian Clarke

✦ *"There's more B.S. in fly fishing than there is in a Kansas feedlot."* Lefty Kreh

✦ *"Fly fishing may be a sport invented by insects with fly fishermen as bait."* P. J. O'Rourke

✦ *"Fly fishing is like sex, everyone thinks there is more than there is, and that everyone is getting more than their share."* Henry Kanemoto

✦ *"Fly making gives us a new sense, almost. We are constantly on the lookout, and view everything with added interest. Possibly we may turn it into a bug of some kind."* Theodore Gordon

✦ *"There is no greater fan of fly fishing than the worm."* Patrick F. McManus

SEEING IS NOT ALWAYS BELIEVING

Whales and dolphins look like fish, live in the water, and swim like fish. However, they are mammals. They breathe air, are warm-blooded, and deliver offspring by live birth. So now you know.

Me, a fish? Don't make me laugh!

BLUEFIN TUNA: BIG AND FAST

❖ The bluefin tuna is one of the fastest and largest of the world's fishes. Its torpedo shape accounts for its speed and endurance. Bluefins are well camouflaged from above and below, being metallic blue on top and silvery white on the bottom.

❖ Their huge appetite makes for an average size of 6 feet (1.8 meters) and 550 pounds (250 kg). The IGFA world record bluefin on a rod and reel was 1,496 pounds (678.58 kg), caught off Nova Scotia. Tuna get big by eating almost constantly—fish, crustaceans, squid, and eels. They even filter-feed on zooplankton and have been known to eat kelp.

❖ Bluefins can live for up to 20 years. They are so big and fast that they suffer few serious threats, especially in warmer waters. However, in the colder waters around Newfoundland, orca whales will drive tuna into bays each September during the tuna's migration, and feed heavily on them.

❖ Atlantic bluefin tuna are warm-blooded—a rarity among fish. In spite of this, they are able to survive in the frigid waters off Newfoundland and Iceland, as well as the much warmer Gulf of Mexico and Mediterranean Sea where they spawn. They are major-league migratory fish, with some having been tracked as they swam from North America to Europe several times a year.

Most Expensive Table Fish

In 2011, a 754-pound (342-kg) bluefin tuna sold in Tokyo's main fish market for 32.49 million yen (around $400,000). It was caught off the coast of northern Japan, an area known for the quality of its tuna. That's $530 per pound or about $100 for a fish sandwich (not including the bun).

Workers processing tuna at a fish market in Tokyo, Japan.

Sushi

Sushi began as fast food in Japan. It was a rolled-up product made with fermented fish or other seafood and rice, wrapped in nori, a type of seaweed. The word "sushi" means sour-tasting and refers to the practice of fermenting the fish. Contemporary sushi remains popular because it is easy and fast to prepare, even though fermented fish is no longer used. Instead, fresh uncooked (or cooked) fish is used. Sushi can also be used as bait.

SASHIMI

In Japan, sashimi refers to a very fresh meat, most commonly fish, sliced into thin pieces. Many years ago, as a culinary process, it was considered too unfavorable to be used by anyone other than the samurai. Contemporary cuisine requires the highest care to make sure that the sashimi is fresh and safe from parasites and other toxins.

Pufferfish: Deadly Cuisine

Pufferfish are the second most poisonous animal in the world, second only to the golden poison frog. Even if death does not occur after eating pufferfish, there is the possibility of a coma lasting several days. Pufferfish are prepared by chefs who know which parts are edible and in what amount. So why would anyone want to risk eating one? Apparently, the uncooked flesh is capable of causing the desired effects of intoxication, light-headedness, and numbness of the tongue and lips. You could have the same effects with 4 ounces of scotch with no threat of coma or death.

Pufferfish

Who's in Charge? Sharks Are

More than three-quarters of the earth is covered by water. Sharks are the apex predators in the ocean, so think of this the next time you go swimming in the sea.

✦ **Eyelids:** Sharks are energetic feeders. Most have a nictitating membrane (from the Latin word "nictare," meaning to blink) that protects the shark's eyes when attacking its prey. The great white shark lacks this membrane and instead rolls its eyes backward to protect them when it strikes its prey. Nictitating membrane or not, if you are in the water and close enough to see a shark's eyes, it's game over.

✦ **Digestion:** Shark digestion takes a long time. Unwanted items may not get past the stomach. Instead, the shark can turn its stomach inside out to eject those unwanted items.

✦ **Buoyancy:** Unlike other fish, sharks do not have swim bladders for buoyancy. Instead, their large liver is filled with lighter-than-water oil. The liver makes up 30 percent of the shark's body mass.

✦ **Teeth:** Shark teeth are not attached to bone because there are no bones in a shark, only cartilage. In order to survive, sharks have developed the ability to replace teeth lost under normal conditions. Sharks have several rows of teeth, and as one tooth is lost, the one behind moves forward to fill the empty space. Some sharks, like the bull shark, can have 50 rows of teeth. Sharks shed teeth throughout their lives, and some produce as many as 35,000 teeth in their lifetime.

A great white shark rolls back its eyes while attacking a baited line.

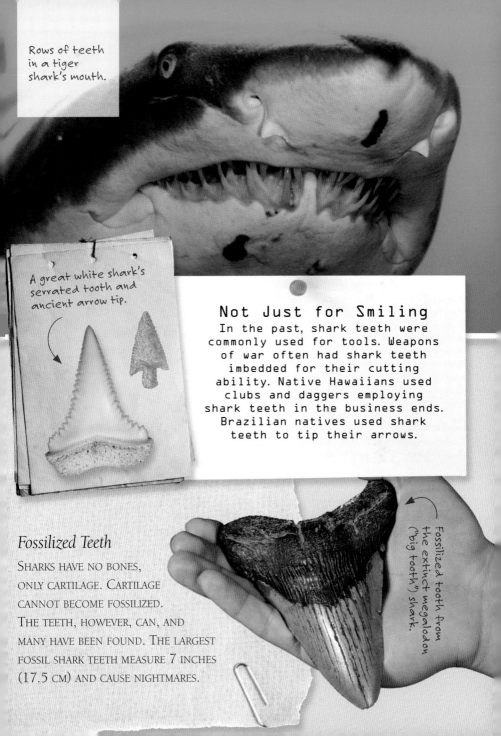

Rows of teeth in a tiger shark's mouth.

A great white shark's serrated tooth and ancient arrow tip.

Not Just for Smiling

In the past, shark teeth were commonly used for tools. Weapons of war often had shark teeth imbedded for their cutting ability. Native Hawaiians used clubs and daggers employing shark teeth in the business ends. Brazilian natives used shark teeth to tip their arrows.

Fossilized Teeth

SHARKS HAVE NO BONES, ONLY CARTILAGE. CARTILAGE CANNOT BECOME FOSSILIZED. THE TEETH, HOWEVER, CAN, AND MANY HAVE BEEN FOUND. THE LARGEST FOSSIL SHARK TEETH MEASURE 7 INCHES (17.5 CM) AND CAUSE NIGHTMARES.

Fossilized tooth from the extinct megalodon ("big tooth") shark.

Plastic worms

Dead Sticking

With this technique, a soft plastic bait is allowed to sit on the bottom for what seems like years as the angler awaits the arrival of a suicidal fish. The strategy is simply to leave the bait alone and allow a cruising fish to find it. The highlight of dead sticking comes when the angler moves the bait slower than might be thought possible, to a slightly different site, mere inches away.

The Popular Plastic Worm

❋ The popularity of this soft plastic fishing lure cannot be denied. It looks and feels realistic, can be infused with any color, and the plastic takes a scent well.

❋ The plastic worm is both effective and versatile. It can be fished at any depth and retrieved at any speed. When rigged with the hook point buried in the worm, it can be fished in heavy cover without risk of it catching on weeds, rocks, or other underwater objects.

❋ The plastic worm is also popular because of its low price. While an angler might be hesitant to throw an expensive plug into a tangled area, he or she would probably be willing to risk an inexpensive plastic worm.

FISHING JIGS

A jig is a hook with a heavy lead head molded onto the hook near the eye. A jig can be fished in several ways. It can be cast or fished vertically below a boat with an up and down jigging motion, usually on or near the bottom. The jig hook is usually dressed with a hook-hiding skirt made of hair or rubber. The hook can also be hidden in a plastic grub or other soft plastic bait. So versatile is the jig that it was often included in survival gear for military pilots during World War II.

Jig

Ribbon tail

Ribbon Tail
The ribbon tail is a soft plastic worm with a long, ribbon-like tail that ripples seductively when retrieved. The advantage of this lure is its action, even when moving very slowly.

Edward Ringwood Hewitt

Hewitt (1866–1957) was an American pioneer in stream reconstruction and trout habitat improvement. He ran his own hatchery and wrote several classic fly-fishing books. Among his many innovations were felt-soled wading shoes (for better grip) and many fly patterns.

The History of Fishing Waders

+ Invented in the 1750s, early waders were made of oilskin—6-ounce (170-gram) Egyptian cotton treated with an oil or wax finish. It was canvas with linseed oil waterproofing. If oil was not available, you could use tallow.

+ Rubber made canvas into effective waders. Vulcanized rubber uses heat in the processing and was named after the Roman god of fire, Vulcan. This process was patented in 1843. However, the first rubberized canvas waders did not start appearing until the early 1900s.

+ Many materials proved to be good for waders and are still available. You can take your pick of canvas, nylon, vinyl, neoprene, or latex. Neoprene, an artificial rubber, was invented in the 1930s and is important for cold weather. It is slightly buoyant and is an excellent insulator.

+ Breathable waders are made from layering Gore-Tex or other similar materials that keep water out while letting sweat and water vapor escape (much to the pleasure of one's fishing companion on a hot day).

What's not to love about a sport involving rubber pants?

Types of Flies

Flies are intended to fool fish into feeding. They are named either for their function or for the natural organism they imitate. Some, like the attractor, look like nothing on God's green earth, but still cause fish to make fools of themselves whenever such a monstrosity floats overhead.

The Coachman is an attractor fly.

ATTRACTORS AND IMITATORS

These are the two general categories of flies. Attractors are flies that do not look like any specific insect. Often made with bright materials, they goad fish into striking. Imitators (also known as deceivers) are flies that are constructed with an eye toward the color, size, and shape of specific natural insects.

✣ **Wet flies:** All stream-borne insects are susceptible to being swept away by river currents. Wet flies mimic these unfortunate individuals. The beard or throat of a wet fly hangs down under the body and represents the legs of the insect.

The Diawl Bach, which is Welsh for little devil, is a wet fly that imitates a midge pupa.

The classic Adams dry fly imitates the mayfly insect.

✣ **Dry flies:** These represent the adult stage of an insect and are tied so that they float on top of the water. Floatability is achieved by using lighter-than-water materials and feathers that spread the weight of the fly over a larger surface area.

Carrie Stevens

★ Carrie Stevens was the wife of a Maine fishing guide. In 1924, she tied some white bucktail under a hook and two long, olive-gray saddle hackles on top to imitate the long, slender smelt. Smelt were the favorite prey fish of salmon and trout in the Rangeley Lake area of Maine.

★ A short time later, she caught a nearly 7-pound (3-kg) brook trout. Her fish won second place in a national magazine contest. Requests for her fly came pouring in, and Carrie was in the fly-tying business.

★ In 1927, she developed the famous Ghost series of smelt fly patterns. In total, she originated over 150 streamer/hairwing patterns, many of which are still in use today.

BEAD HEADS

Nymph flies that have a metal bead at the head are designed to be heavy enough to get deep to where the fish are holding. Shiny beads can also be used to attract fish by imitating the gas bubble that many emerging nymphs use to aid their rise to the water's surface.

✤ **Nymphs and emergers:** A nymph represents the early phase of a hatching insect, usually found low in the water column. Emergers mimic the late phase of a stream-borne insect, caught in the film surface as it changes into the winged adult form.

Crystal Prince is a nymph fly with a bead head.

The Munro killer is a hairwing fly.

✤ **Streamers and hairwings:** These both mimic small baitfish, but streamers primarily use long feathers to represent the narrow fish bodies, while hairwings (also known as bucktails) use animal hair. The name bucktail comes from the original natural material used—hair from the tail of a buck deer—which can be dyed many colors.

Walleye caught on a jig with a plastic worm.

PUTTING THE "EYE" IN WALLEYE

The walleye's eyes have a prominent reflective layer that allows them to see in low light conditions. This reflective layer also makes them light-sensitive. As a result, they prefer to feed in deep water, which gives them a great advantage over their prey.

On the Watch for Walleye

Sometimes called the perch pike, the walleye is really a member of the perch family. It is favored as a table fish because of its mild flavor, and it appears on the menu of many restaurants.

★ **Life cycle:** The walleye lays its eggs on a gravel bar, without the benefit of a nest. These rapidly growing fish will attain a length of 4 to 6 inches (10 to 15 cm) between late spring and late summer. This rate of growth continues for the next four years until it declines. Upon attaining 10 inches (25 cm), the walleye's diet switches entirely to minnows. After walleyes mature, they must eat continually just to maintain themselves. They continue to grow for their entire life, and they accomplish this by hearty eating habits.

★ **Habitat:** These denizens of large lakes prefer depths of more than 10 feet (3 meters). They prefer the colder water at these depths, and their light-sensitive eyes require the lower brightness. Walleye will feed in shallower water, but only in the dark of night or when a surface chop prevents sunshine from penetrating too deeply.

★ **Feeding habits:** Midday, walleye stay in dark areas found in the 15- to 25-foot (4.6- to 7.6-meter) depths. They also feed at night, and can cover a large lake in their nocturnal wanderings. They are fast swimmers, thanks to the slender shape of their body, and can easily overcome their prey. Those they catch are held fast by the walleye's sharp teeth. Under low light conditions, the walleye bite more. On sunny days, they may feed only at dusk and dawn, but on cloudy days, they may feed all day and all night.

The not-so-speedy seahorse.

World's Slowest Fish

Seahorses are the slowest in all of fishdom. There are more than 30 species, and their top speed is a blistering 0.001 miles per hour. At this speed, it takes a seahorse an hour to swim 5 feet (1.5 meters).

RED DRUM

Back in the 1980s, the "blackened redfish" craze nearly meant the end of this species. Its alternative name of red drum comes from the vocalization that the fish makes when in trouble. The sound is produced by vibrations in its swim bladder. The most distinguishing characteristic is the single black spot on its tail. Of special interest to anglers is the red drum's willingness to take almost any kind of bait, lure, or fly. These fish come into such shallow water that anglers can wade and cast to feeding fish—the fish do headstands as they feed, with the head down in the grass and the tail sticking out of the water.

Got Your Ears On?

Fish have no ears but are very adept at sensing movement and vibration. The organ responsible for this is the lateral line, a series of receptors running from the gills to the tail. Some receptors are specialized for pressure sensitivity, while others are electrical receptors and may aid in migration.

Lateral line

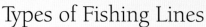

Types of Fishing Lines

+ The earliest fishing lines were made of braided, or furled, horsehair or silk. Casting was not a consideration because the earliest lines were the same length as the rod.

+ Later, when fishing reels became common, braided lines of longer length were made from cordage or cotton twine. These were similar to the materials used for a ship's rigging but much lighter.

+ As the variety of reels grew, each required a different kind of line. Cotton twine remained common for bait casting, while linseed-oil-covered silk was used for fly casting.

+ In 1938, American chemical company DuPont announced the invention of nylon and, in 1939, they started selling nylon monofilament fishing line. The effectiveness of spinning reels was greatly improved with nylon lines, which remain popular even today.

Braided fishing line

A reel of strong braided line for saltwater fishing.

+ Modern fly-fishing lines have a braided core and are covered by a buoyant coating that requires none of the maintenance of the older braided silk lines.

Monofilament and Multifilament

♦ **Nylon monofilament** is the most commonly used of all fishing lines, because it is cheap, translucent, and available in many strengths. It can be made to be abrasive-resistant, low-stretch, or resistant to taking a set (retaining its shape) after being stored for a long period of time.

♦ **Multifilament** is a braided line made of several strands of polyethylene. It does not stretch and is more sensitive than monofilament line. It is claimed to be five to ten times stronger than steel of comparable construction. However, since no one uses steel lines, it would seem to be a moot point.

Test

Test is not a quiz, but the breaking strength of a line. Larger fish require heavier lines, and smaller fish can be fooled with lighter lines. Commercially made lines vary from less than a pound to a hundred pound test (0.45 to 45 kg), or more— that is more than enough varieties to cover every angler's needs.

LEADER LINES

* A leader is a heavy piece of line attached at the end of the main fishing line. Its purpose is to avoid breaking the mainline when a toothy critter takes the bait.

* The purpose of the leader on a fly line is to taper the thick fly line down to a thin end so that a fly can be attached. A thin leader is less likely to be seen and avoided by the fish, but it is also more likely to be broken by a heavy fish.

* Two types of fly leaders are available commercially. First is a knotless, tapered leader, which starts out as a piece of heavy monofilament. Partway down its length, it is drawn through a reducing die so that the diameter becomes smaller. Moving farther down, the leader is drawn through a smaller reducing die. The process is repeated until the end is of the desired diameter.

* The second option is to tie short pieces of smaller and smaller monofilament in succession until the leader end has the desired thickness. The standard formula is 75 percent thick butt section, 10 percent intermediate hinge section, and 25 percent thin tippet.

Fear Knot

Even before making his or her first cast, the angler must learn to tie the hook to the line. Every angler knows several knots. In truth, anglers need only a few but, like many other things in fishing, it got out of control and gets worse every year. Each slight variation has its own name. Commonly used knots include:

+ Blood
+ Clinch
+ Needle
+ Palomar
+ Rapala
+ San Diego jam
+ Snell
+ Surgeon's
+ Uni
+ Water

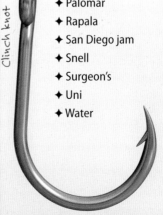

Monofilament line

Clinch knot

Record Catches

The International Game Fish Association (IGFA) lists more than 1,200 record fish in the all-tackle category. Records are for all types of angling and from around the world. Here are a few:

+ Albacore
88 lb 2 oz (39.97 kg)

+ Amberjack, greater
156 lb 13 oz (71.15 kg)

+ Barbel
13 lb 8 oz (6.12 kg)

+ Barracuda, great
85 lb 0 oz (38.55 kg)

+ Barramundi
98 lb 6 oz (44.64 kg)

+ Bass, largemouth
22 lb 4 oz (10.12 kg and 10.09 kg—dual record holders)

+ Bass, smallmouth
11 lb 15 oz (5.41 kg)

+ Bass, spotted
10 lb 4 oz (4.65 kg)

+ Bass, striped
81 lb 14 oz (37.14 kg)

+ Bluefish
31 lb 12 oz (14.4 kg)

+ Bluegill
4 lb 12 oz (2.15 kg)

+ Bonefish
19 lb 0 oz (8.61 kg)

+ Bonito, Atlantic
18 lb 4 oz (8.3 kg)

+ Bonito, Australian
20 lb 11 oz (9.4 kg)

+ Bream
13 lb 3 oz (6.01 kg)

+ Bullhead, black
7 lb 7 oz (3.37 kg)

+ Bullhead, brown
7 lb 6 oz (3.35 kg)

+ Bullhead, yellow
6 lb 6 oz (2.89 kg)

+ Burbot
25 lb 2 oz (11.4 kg)

+ Carp, common
75 lb 11 oz (34.35 kg)

+ Catfish, blue
143 lb 0 oz (64.86 kg)

+ Catfish, channel
58 lb 0 oz (26.3 kg)

+ Catfish, flathead
123 lb 0 oz (55.79 kg)

+ Catfish, white
19 lb 5 oz (8.78 kg)

+ Char, Arctic
32 lb 9 oz (14.77 kg)

+ Cod, Atlantic
98 lb 12 oz (44.79 kg)

+ Cod, Pacific
38 lb 9 oz (17.5 kg)

+ Crappie, black
5 lb 0 oz (2.26 kg)

+ Crappie, white
5 lb 3 oz (2.35 kg)

+ Dolphin or dolphinfish
87 lb 0 oz (39.46 kg)

+ Drum, black
113 lb 1 oz (51.28 kg)

+ Drum, red
94 lb 2 oz (42.69 kg)

+ Eel, American
9 lb 4 oz (4.21 kg)

+ Eel, European
7 lb 14 oz (3.6 kg)

+ Flounder, summer
22 lb 7 oz (10.17 kg)

+ Flounder, winter
7 lb 0 oz (3.17 kg)

+ Gar, alligator
279 lb 0 oz (126.55 kg)

+ Gar, longnose
50 lb 0 oz (22.68 kg)

+ Goldfish, Asian
3 lb 9 oz (1.62 kg)

+ Grayling
4 lb 12 oz (2.18 kg)

+ Grayling, Arctic
5 lb 15 oz (2.69 kg)

+ Grouper, black
124 lb 0 oz (56.24 kg)

+ Grouper, gag
80 lb 6 oz (36.46 kg)

+ Grouper, goliath
680 lb 0 oz (308.44 kg)

+ Grouper, red
42 lb 4 oz (19.16 kg)

+ Grouper, yellowfin
42 lb 0 oz (19.05 kg)

+ Hake, European
15 lb 9 oz (7.08 kg)

(continued on page 103)

Bass Feeding Facts

+ **Predator, not hunter:** Take a close look at a big bass and you will find a large mouth and even larger belly— definitely not the form of a swift hunting fish. Bass prefer live food sources such as live baitfish. However, they do not hunt for their dinner. Instead, they lie in wait to ambush the unwary lunch that happens to swim by unaware of its imminent fate. Bass will not hang around forever where there are no baitfish. They will mosey over to another ambush point and take up residence.

+ **Feeding temperature:** Like the vast majority of fish, bass are cold-blooded. As their environment changes, so do their behaviors. Even involuntary bodily functions are affected. Most important is metabolism. Bass are most active between 60 and 70°F (15 and 21°C). Below 50°F (10°C), they seek food infrequently. When water temperatures exceed 80°F (27°C), low oxygen levels stress bass and they do not expend energy on feeding.

+ **In the zone:** Bass position themselves so that they can charge their prey from below and behind. This instinct probably evolved as a function of success over time. The tail is the main propulsion driver, and this means that the strike zone is going to be ahead of the bass. Bass cannot swim backward, so a straight-ahead charge, starting below the prey, makes sense.

+ **Present an easy meal:** Anglers can take advantage of the bass's sloth and instincts by presenting their lures to imitate a happy-go-lucky, naive baitfish. Such presentations will trigger the bass's feeding behavior because it represents an easy meal.

A largemouth bass waiting for an unwary baitfish to swim by.

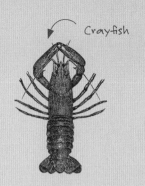
Crayfish

BASS FOODS

The list of available bass foods is a long one:
- Crayfish (top choice)
- Shad
- Rats
- Mice
- Frogs
- Snakes
- Salamanders
- Worms
- Lizards
- Grubs
- Bait-fish
- Insects
- Leeches
- Ducklings—yes, little duckies, and just about anything else you can think of.

Leech
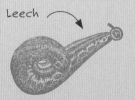

Flipping for Bass

When bass are hiding in heavy cover, an underhand pitching cast called flipping can accurately deliver the lure quietly into small open spaces. It is delivered on a short line and often results in immediate strikes as the lure quietly drops in above the fish. The fish, apparently, does not question the dinner that has just dropped from the heavens into its lair.

THE STRIKE ZONE

Predatory fish such as bass are strong visual feeders. The size of the target must also be taken into account. For example, although under optimal conditions bass may be able to see 50 feet (15 meters) away, to chase a small lure at this distance is not efficient in terms of return on investment for the energy required. So how do they decide what to ambush? Every predatory fish has its own reaction distance within which it has a higher probability of success. This is known as the strike zone. This charge distance is instinctive. Bait outside of the zone will be passed up.

The Early Course of Coarse Fishing

✤ Although Britain is blessed with many fishing opportunities, angling was originally afforded only to the gentry. Those privileged ones disdained anything but game fishing. The rest they thought to be uncouth, or coarse.

✤ As a continuing tradition, game fishing is reserved for those who can afford to pay the hefty fees. Rather than resort to mayhem, those priced out of game fishing developed the practice of coarse fishing.

✤ Contemporary coarse anglers are dedicated and very knowledgeable in the ways of their prey. They are also staunch conservationists and adhere to a strict code of catch and release to ensure the future of their sport.

IT'S ALL JUST FISHING

In the United States, there is no distinction between game and coarse fishing—it's all just fishing. Fishing is also allowed just about everywhere, with very few "pay-to-fish" situations.

Game Fishing

The common definition of game fishing in Britain includes Atlantic salmon, brown trout, sea trout, and rainbow trout. Grayling also belong to the salmon family but count as coarse fish. In addition, trout waters are usually restricted to fly fishing. The cost for game fishing remains too high for most anglers.

TYPES OF "COARSE" FISHING

The main techniques are float fishing, ledgering, and spinning.

★ In **float fishing**, the bait is suspended under a float made of hollow plastic (or wood or quill). This method is the simplest, and is a good way for the novice to gain experience.

★ **Ledgering** is bottom fishing using a weight but no float. The weight holds the bait on the bottom of the river or lake, with hopes that a hungry fish will swim by. The technique of bouncing bait along the bottom in a river's current is known as a rolling ledger.

★ **Spinning** employs a lure or a live baitfish retrieved through the water.

Arctic Grayling: Miniature Sailfish

The distinguishing characteristic of this cold-water fish is its large dorsal fin. Anglers use flies, spinning lures, and natural bait to catch these lavender-colored schooling fish.

FISHY QUOTES

✦ *"All Americans believe that they are born fishermen. For a man to admit distaste for fishing would be like denouncing mother-love and hating moonlight."* John Steinbeck

✦ *"I still don't know why I fish or why other men fish, except that we like it and it makes us think and feel."* Roderick L. Haig-Brown

✦ *"The solution to any problem—work, love, money, whatever—is to go fishing, and the worse the problem, the longer the trip should be."* John Gierach

✦ *"Of course, folk fish for different reasons. There are enough aspects of angling to satisfy the aspirations of people remarkably unalike."* Maurice Wiggin

✦ *"If all the reasons for going a-fishing that mankind has ever put forth were packed into a great compendium they would simmer down to one single reason... It's like falling in love—they can't help it."* William Sherwood Fox

✦ *"Herbert Hoover said [fishing] was for fun, and to wash your soul, and I don't say he was altogether wrong, but I can't forget that he was less than altogether right about a number of things."* Arnold Gingrich

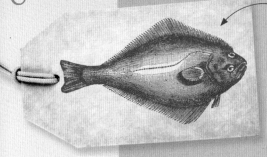

ATLANTIC HALIBUT: BIG, FAT FLATTY

This largest member of the flatfish family prefers the coast of Norway for spawning. Juveniles live in relatively shallow water, but adults stay at depths of 300 to 2,000 yards (or meters). Atlantic halibut is highly prized as a table fish because of its tasty, firm, white meat.

FISH OF A THOUSAND DINNERS

According to the World Records Academy, Gunther Hansel's 482-pound 13-ounce (219-kg) halibut caught near the West Fjords in Iceland set a new record, besting a 464-pound (210-kg) fish caught off Norway in 2009. Hansel's halibut was sold to a fish market for about $4,000. Halibut caught by commercial boats can reach 700 pounds (317 kg).

Mako shark

Some Fly Records

♦ Caught off the coast of California in 2009, an 11-foot (3.4-meter), 600-pound (272-kg) mako shark is believed to be the largest fish caught on a fly rod—yet another reason to stay out of the water.

♦ According to the Guinness World Records, the most species caught on a fly rod in one year by a single person was 85—most likely an unemployed person.

The catch from a halibut fishing trip, with a clear winner for largest fish.

Fish suspended over smoldering wood shavings in a smokehouse.

Smoked Fish

SMOKING IS A FORM OF PRESERVATION AND HAS BEEN PRACTICED SINCE BEFORE RECORDED HISTORY. IT PERMITS SAFE TRANSPORT OF FISH BY STOPPING THE NATURAL BACTERIAL BREAKDOWN PROCESS. THE SMOKED PRODUCT REMAINS EDIBLE FOR EXTENDED PERIODS OF TIME. NOWADAYS, SMOKING IS USUALLY DONE FOR FLAVOR AND TEXTURE RATHER THAN PRESERVATION.

Black Bass Records

✤ On June 22nd, 1932, American angler George Perry caught his IGFA world record 22-pound 4-ounce (10.09-kg) largemouth bass in Montgomery Lake in Georgia.

✤ Manaby Kurita became dual world record holder when he caught a largemouth bass in Lake Biwa, Japan, in 2009. Although both fish are listed as weighing the same in pounds and ounces, Kurita's fish was 10.12 kg, making it marginally heavier.

✤ Dave Romero of Long Island, NY, caught 3,001 bass in 77 days in 1984. He averaged 38 to 40 fish per day for 77 days.

Haddock Secrets

✦ Haddock live off both American and European Atlantic coasts and are highly valued as table fare.

✦ Like other members of the cod family, haddock can be distinguished from other saltwater fish by its three dorsal fins.

✦ One female may release 3 million eggs each spawn.

✦ Traditionally, this fish is marketed with the skin on so that consumers can be sure they are getting the haddock they want.

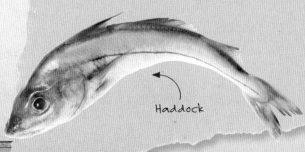

Haddock

I'LL FLY AWAY

Some fish swim, some walk, some jump, and some fly. Flying fish are native to warm tropical and subtropical waters of the Atlantic, Pacific, and Indian oceans. Using their broad fins, they build up speed, leap from the water, and glide above the surface as a way to avoid predators. Flights of 4 feet (1.2 meters) above the surface are typical. By flapping its tail on the surface, the flying fish can extend its "flight" and remain above the surface. The close proximity of predator fish encourages longer flights.

Flying fish

The Fast and the Shallow

Fast fish need more oxygen than slower fish. Oxygen is more plentiful near the surface than in the depths. For this reason, fish like marlin and tuna spend more time swimming closer to the surface than do grouper, which live on the bottom.

THE SPEEDY WAHOO

This speedster of the tropical and temperate seas is fast enough to feed on 43-miles-per-hour (69-kph) flying fish. Slower prey includes herring, lanternfish, mackerel, and squid. The wahoo is often a loner, and frequently ventures far out into mid-ocean areas. Its migrations take it from the mid-Atlantic states in the north to Columbia in the south. Wahoo take advantage of the Gulf Stream to facilitate their travels. The Straits of Florida are their favored location.

THE JACKSON HOLE (WYOMING) ONE-FLY EVENT

The rules are simple—you have one fly; it cannot be changed; if it is lost, you are out. Whoever catches the most/biggest trout wins. This annual three-day event benefits trout and trout habitat. Its purpose is to raise funds for conservation projects, and it draws fly fishermen from around the world.

HOW TO MAKE A BAMBOO ROD

Bamboo—actually a grass, not a wood—is prized as a rod-making material because of its beauty, flexibility, and strength. Making a bamboo rod is a hand process using specialist tools and, as a result, bamboo rods are expensive. The basic process is:

❶ Split a stalk, or culm, of bamboo lengthwise into many narrow strips. Plane each strip to remove the hard outer layer.

❷ Plane each strip lengthwise so that it forms an equilateral triangle in cross-section. When six strips are placed together, they will form a rod that is hexagonal in cross-section.

❸ Plane each triangular strip lengthwise so that it tapers from the handle end of the rod to the rod tip. The thinner end will be more flexible than the thicker end. The formula defining the taper determines how flexible or stiff the rod will be.

❹ Glue six triangular stips together to form a hexagonal rod. To create a longer rod, use metal ferrules to join several sections together.

❺ Attach rod eyes and other hardware to complete the rod.

Bamboo fishing rod

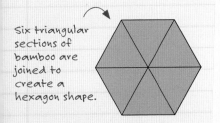

Six triangular sections of bamboo are joined to create a hexagon shape.

HOUSE OF HARDY

In the 1870s, William and John Hardy started as gun makers in Alnwick in the northeast of England. By 1880, bamboo had become popular for rod making and the Hardys invented a system for building hexagonal rods from bamboo. Hardy rods won gold medals in exhibitions every year until medals were no longer presented.

In 1891, the Hardy Perfect reel was invented and, with only minor changes, is still in production. As proof of the highest quality of Hardy products, the company was awarded ten royal warrants. In 1907, John Hardy published *Salmon Fishing*, considered to be the most complete listing of full-dress salmon flies ever written. The House of Hardy continues to operate from its original location of Alnwick.

Carp-catching Considerations

Carp fishing represents the epitome of patience. These fish are not aggressive strikers and they do not stalk their prey.

+ While the common carp often attains 20 pounds (9 kg), it can weigh up to 80 pounds (36 kg) and live 50 years. However, on average, smaller carp weigh 2 to 5 pounds (0.9 to 2.3 kg) and live for 15 years. For the little tiddlers, ultra-light spinning gear or even fly-fishing tackle works fine. However, most carp fishing requires medium-weight tackle and lines of 8 to 10 pounds (3.6 to 4.5 kg).

+ Carp prefer bait such as corn kernels, worms, or dough balls. For the giant, economy-sized carp, try large crayfish. Carp are spooky by nature, especially when in shallow water. For bigger carp, fish the deeper pools and backwaters.

+ While rigging up with a few kernels of corn on a single hook, broadcast corn into the area you will be fishing. A slip sinker is important because carp are gentle feeders and will drop a baited hook if they feel any resistance. Freshen the area with more corn each time you catch a fish because the carp may have eaten all the broadcast corn, leaving nothing behind to attract another carp.

HAIR RIG

A hair rig works well for cagey carp. A hair rig suspends a small bait from the bare hook by a thin nylon "hair," preventing the fish from feeling the hook until the bait is taken deep and it is too late to drop it.

Fisherman with a large common carp.

A Common Carp by Any Other Name...

Take your pick: common carp, European carp, French carp, Italian carp, German carp, Israeli carp, leather carp, mirror carp, king carp, koi, sewer bass, buglemouth. Whatever you call it, the common carp was brought to North America in 1831. Long a food fish in Asia, it has not caught on as table fare.

ELECTRONIC BITE ALARM

Used by many carp anglers, this battery-operated device sounds off when the smallest amount of line movement is detected. It would also make a nice addition to a cookie jar for families with young children.

Largest Ice-fishing Competition

Gull Lake near Brainerd, Minnesota, claims to host the world's largest ice-fishing competition. Each January, 15,000 anglers compete for cash and other prizes. However, in Hwacheon, South Korea, nearly a million people attend the ice-fishing festival every January, although only thousands (estimated to be more than 10,000) take part in the actual competition. Perhaps the lack of participation is explained by the fact that bare hands are used to catch the fish. No records are reported for frostbite.

Participants in an ice-fishing competition in Russia.

WHAT'S IN A NAME? SOMETHING SOUNDS FISHY

Consumers can be fussy. Some original fish names are less than appetizing, so marketers are renaming fish to encourage buyers to take some home. Here are a few old and new names:

Old Name	New Name
Pilchards	Cornish sardines
Slimehead	Orange roughy
Patagonian toothfish	Chilean sea bass
Rockfish	Pacific red snapper
Dogfish	Rock salmon
Witchfish	Torbay sole

Dogfish or rock salmon— which sounds tastier?

Full-dress Salmon Flies

Once upon a time, the British Empire extended worldwide. It was often said, at least by fly tyers, that the sun never sets on the British source of fly-tying materials. As a result, British salmon anglers designed beautiful flies from exquisite plumage. It was not uncommon for these flies to require 20 or more different materials. This tradition is kept alive by a handful of full-dress salmon tyers, who strive to copy the original flies by using the original materials. Unfortunately, some of the materials are in very short supply, and some species are now extinct or endangered. Serious full-dress tyers are constantly on the lookout for these materials and are willing to pay the high prices demanded for them.

Virtually every contemporary full-dress salmon fly will become a treasured artistic piece, framed for display and never to be fished.

A matched pair of bustard feathers for a full-dress salmon fly can cost $50 to $800, depending on the species. Can you say "utter nonsense"?

Nothing in Moderation

During the time when full-dress salmon flies were intended to be fished, the materials list got out of hand. Here is the materials list for the classic Jock Scott:

- Silver twist
- Light yellow floss
- Indian crow
- Black herl
- Silver tinsel
- Toucan feathers
- Black silk
- Black hackle
- Silver lace
- Silver tinsel
- Gallina
- Black turkey
- Bustard
- Gray mallard
- Golden pheasant
- Peacock
- Red macaw
- Red- and yellow-dyed swan
- Mallard
- Jungle cock
- Chatterer
- Blue macaw

Jock Scott fly from George Kelson's book "The Salmon Fly," 1895.

Some of the materials used in old fly patterns may come from species that are now endangered or even extinct. When the Jock Scott was invented in Britain in the 1890s, long before species were endangered, many of the species available to British fly tyers came from their colonies around the world. There was no such thing as prohibited species. Nowadays, possession of such materials is sometimes still permitted if documentation proves that the material was collected prior to the prohibition.

Salmon Fly-tying Luminaries

❖ **Captain Hale:** Hale's book *How to Tie Salmon Flies* (1892) represents the zenith of salmon fly-tying practices. The book was intended to be the authority for describing how to tie and what materials to use. His writing is consulted to this day.

❖ **George Kelson:** George Kelson's book, *The Salmon Fly—How to Dress It and How to Use It*, was published in 1895. It is considered one of the finest works on tying salmon flies. Kelson's book is much sought after by book collectors and it commands a premium price.

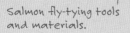

Salmon fly-tying tools and materials.

Fishing Plugs

A plug is an artificial lure made out of wood, plastic, or metal that is designed to imitate the prey of predatory fish. Plugs began as lures for bass, but were found to be effective for other fish as well.

wobbler

+ **Invention:** The modern concept of the plug lure is attributed to James Heddon from Dowagiac, Michigan. He was whittling a piece of wood one day in the late 1890s and tossed the carved piece into a pond, where it was taken by a black bass. His observation led him to experiment with several designs. He finally perfected his design and the Lucky 13 became the first commercial bass plug.

+ **Construction:** Much thought is put into building an effective plug design. Some designs attempt to mimic natural food sources. Others resemble nothing in nature, but produce a swimming action that brings fish up from the depths as they investigate the commotion.

+ **Actions:** Some plugs float, while others suspend with neutral buoyancy. Many are designed to dive when retrieved (cranked in) and are known as crankbait. Those that swim from side to side are called wobblers. If a plug has a lip, the size of the lip determines whether the plug will dive deep or run shallow. The variety of plug actions is huge and that accounts for the very large number of different types of plugs on the market today.

TYPICAL PLUG CONSTRUCTION

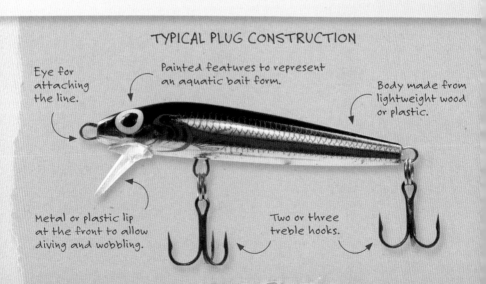

Eye for attaching the line.

Painted features to represent an aquatic bait form.

Body made from lightweight wood or plastic.

Metal or plastic lip at the front to allow diving and wobbling.

Two or three treble hooks.

Fishing plugs were once carved from barrel plugs.

WHY IS A PLUG CALLED A PLUG?

The earliest lure carvers wanted to start with wood that was already shaped roughly like their finished product. Such wood would reduce the production time. They soon discovered that a wooden barrel bung, or plug, was just what they needed. The cylindrical barrel plugs fit the bill and the name stuck like an oversized plug in an undersized bung hole.

COLLECTABLE WOODEN LURES

Long ago, lures were hand-carved from wood. They would get beaten up by fish and were expendable. Eventually, they were replaced by more durable plastic lures. Collectors prize the older wooden variety and pay hefty prices for those in good condition. In 1998, $9,800 was paid for a 1903 Heddon Underwater Minnow. Other collectable lures include:

- Arbogast Sunfish
- Big O
- Bomber
- Crazy Crawler
- Creek Chub Wiggler
- Dowagiac series
- Flatfish
- Hellbender
- Hula Popper
- Jitterbug
- Keeling Expert Minnow
- Lazy Ike
- Moonlight Zig-Zag
- Pflueger's Electric Minnow
- Pikaroon
- Pikie Minnow
- Shakespeare Revolution Bait
- South Bend Minnow
- Worden Wooden Minnow

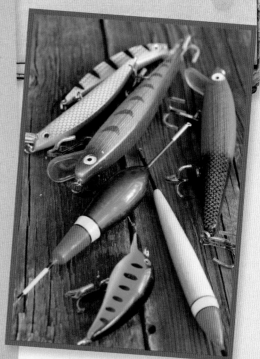

A set of old wooden lures and floats.

TYPES OF SINKERS

Also known as a plummet or weight, a fishing sinker is used to anchor a bait and/or add casting distance. Sinkers vary from a fraction of an ounce to several pounds. Their shape depends on their function. Here are some common types:

★ **Pyramid sinkers** are named for their shape. They are used to hold bottom and present the bait to bottom-feeding fish.

★ **Bullet sinkers** are also named for their shape. They have a hole drilled all the way through them. Line runs through this hole, allowing the weight to hold bottom while the line is free to play out as a fish picks up the bait.

★ **Bank sinkers** are long ovals with a hole in one end to receive the line.

★ **Barrel sinkers**, also called egg sinkers, have a hole for attaching the line. This shape of sinker is effective in holding on a rocky bottom.

★ **Dipsey sinkers** are egg-shaped and are attached to the fishing line via a brass wire loop embedded in the lead.

★ **Split shot** are small, round weights with a cut running halfway through the weight. The split allows them to be crimped onto a line as well as to be removed easily.

Split shot

Sinkers come in numerous shapes, weights, and materials.

FISHY QUOTES

✦ *"Not everything about fishing is noble and reasonable and sane…Fishing is not an escape from life, but often a deeper immersion into it, all of it. The good and the awful, the joyous and the miserable, the comic, the embarrassing, the tragic and the sorrowful."* Harry Middleton

✦ *"The charm of fishing is that it is the pursuit of what is elusive, but obtainable, a perpetual series of occasions for hope."* John Buchan

✦ *"Lovers, poets, religious madmen, and anglers…have this in common—they live for the impassioned anticipation of an uncertain thing."* Ted Leeson

✦ *"We are haunted day and night by the knowledge that the amount of time we spend fishing is inconsequential in comparison with the amount of time we spend doing things we do not love."* Howell Raines

FREESTONE RIVERS AND SPRING CREEKS

❖ Most creeks (small streams) and rivers are of the freestone variety. When seen from a great altitude, freestone creeks look like tree branches, with tiny tributaries combining to make up larger branches and, finally, the main stem. Freestone streams are valued by anglers, and tracking the stream's health is a significant habitat-protective activity.

❖ Spring creeks, on the other hand, spring from the ground at full force. The constant temperature of spring creeks allows for fishing year-round, because they do not get cold enough to freeze in the winter or too hot in the summer.

Trotline Fishing

When trotline fishing, a baited line is tied to a springy tree branch. As a fish takes the bait, it pulls against the branch. The branch springs back and secures the hook in the fish's mouth. Shaking branches indicate a successful hook-up. In practice, the baits can be spread over a larger area by using branches on several trees, with the fisherman sitting back and watching for quaking foliage. Trotlines are not legal for use in all areas. Some places restrict the use of trotlines to saltwater fishing and some restrict the kind of bait used.

WATER FLOW
The water flow at this dam is 400 cubic feet (11 cubic meters) per second. This flow is ten times the ideal flow—extreme fishing!

Pike: Wolves of the Water

Pike are a group of carnivorous predatory fish. They are most often found alone, hunting in warm-water shallows, in or near weed beds.

+ **Characteristics:** Pike have long, slender bodies and duck-shaped mouths full of needle-sharp teeth made for grasping and holding fish. Pike are very variable in size. The smallest, the redfin pickerel, seldom weighs a pound (0.45 kg). At the other end of the family line is the muskellunge, which can reach 70 pounds (32 kg).

+ **Feeding habits:** Pike have a voracious appetite. Among freshwater fish, they are the most piscivorous (fish-eating). Should fish not be available, they will dine on frogs, mice, ducks, and muskrats. The pike's shape, color, and eating methods support its rapacious character. Pike feed by waiting in ambush among the weeds. The pike bends its body into a shallow "S" and unleashes the bend to capture the prey sideways in its mouth. After returning to its hideaway, it swallows the fish headfirst. With its large mouth, a pike can swallow prey one-third to one-half

its own length. If the prey is too large to go down the gullet all at once, the pike swims around with the back end sticking out of its mouth while the front half is digested in its stomach.

+ **Spawning:** Pike do not build nests. Instead, they simply broadcast their eggs and spawn in any available warm-water shallows. Their eggs are adhesive and stick wherever they land. Eggs hatch out in 8 to 15 days. Three to four weeks later, the hatchlings begin cannibalizing their fry mates. So much for brotherly love. It pays to hatch early.

Fastest Freshwater Fish

CLOCKED AT 20 MILES PER HOUR (32 KPH) WHEN CHASING ITS LUNCH, THE PIKE IS THE RECORD HOLDER FOR FASTEST FRESHWATER FISH.

Is that a gander over there? Hey, come closer. I just want to talk, really...

FISHING FOR PIKE (THE NORMAL WAY)

Being among the most aggressive of all freshwater fish, pike can be found near weed beds, lurking, ready to ambush the unwary. They will strike almost any lure or bait—spoons, spinners, plugs, and minnows will all provoke a strike. The larger varieties of pike require use of a wire leader, lest the pike shear through monofilament line. Needle-nose pliers will make unhooking pike less dangerous for the angler.

Northern pike caught on a large plug lure.

FISH SHOOTING

Shooting fish with a rifle is a tradition that has survived in Vermont in the northeast of the United States and nowhere else. Fish hunters climb into trees in spring-flooded areas of Lake Champlain. Their quarry is spawning pike. Experienced fish hunters know that the best shot is one that hits close to a fish. The impact stuns the fish and the pike is collected before it can recover. A direct hit renders the fish too mushy for the table. The sport is an endangered species because the influx of new Vermonters is opposed to what they say is a savagely dangerous practice. For the record, no one has ever been injured by errant bullets.

Falling out of a tree because of the rifle's recoil is, however, not all that uncommon.

Are you insane? I'm not going near those teeth!

Gander Fishing

In Lochmaben in Scotland, pike were often caught with the aid of a gander. A line was tied to a gander's leg. Attached to the line was a hook and live frog. The perturbed gander was then released on the lake. Sooner or later, the gander would cross paths with a pike and battle would commence. The outcome depended on the relative size of the pike and gander.

Birds of a Feather

The plumage of virtually every bird species can be used for fly tying. Feathers are desirable because they give the appearance of bulk without adding weight. The illusion of bulk makes for a fly that is easy to cast while having a "meaty" appearance. Each type of feather is selected for its color, sheen, and fiber length. Some have been popular since fly tying began, while others have come to be used as substitutes for extinct or protected species.

Golden pheasant

Peacock herl feather fiber

Marabou

Hen hackles

HACKLES

More time is spent by fly tyers in the search for high-quality hackle than for any other material. Hackle is found on the neck of a bird. The hackle from a cock has long, thin springy fibers that help a dry fly to float on the water's surface. Hen hackles are softer than cock hackles. They soak up water and move enticingly in the water, adding lifelike movement to wet flies and nymphs.

Palmering a Hackle

This is the technique of wrapping a feather around a hook shank so that each fiber sticks out at 90 degrees to the shank. The advantage of palmering is that it gives the appearance of bulk without adding weight.

Cul de Canard

French for "butt of the duck," these feathers are found near the duck's oily preening gland and have superior ability to float fishing flies.

SOME POPULAR FEATHERS

- Blackbird
- Crow
- Cul de canard
- Duck
- Emu
- Gadwall
- Goose
- Grouse
- Guinea hen
- Hen
- Jungle cock
- Mallard
- Marabou
- Ostrich
- Partridge
- Peacock
- Pheasant
- Rooster
- Starling
- Teal
- Turkey
- Wood duck

FEATHERS ARE IN FASHION

Hackle feathers are used in fly tying. These long, soft feathers are also big news in women's hair extensions. Feathers that once cost a few dollars are now demanding $20 and a war is brewing. Some producers raise 80,000 roosters per year. These are genetically bred for long, strong feathers. The hackle farms are unable to keep up with the current fashion demand. Some tyers recognize that this is a fad and are awaiting the glut of unwanted hackles once this fashion trend goes bust. Other hardcore tyers are predicting the end of the world. Only time will tell.

Stages of an Angler

Most anglers go through a progressive set of stages, defined by the level of desired success. It is possible to be fixated at any stage, as well as to move in either direction between stages. It is also possible that whoever created this list did not know what he or she was talking about. The lesson? There is none. Just get out there and fish. These alleged stages are:

1) Catch a fish.
2) Catch many fish.
3) Catch big fish.
4) Catch a specific fish.

Stage 1

Fish from the Sky

Reports of fish falling from the sky have been around for at least 2,000 years. One of the earliest references is in *The Travels of Peter Mundy in Europe and Asia*, Volume 3 (1634). Apparently, this was a regular occurrence, which he describes as they "dropp out of the ayre." It was also mentioned in Izaak Walton's *Compleat Angler* (1653). Waterspouts—essentially over-water tornadoes—are believed to be responsible for this version of flying fish. With winds up to 200 miles per hour (320 kph), the waterspout can lift fish and even sailboats into the air. The fish are dropped when rain falls from the clouds supporting the waterspout.

Waterspouts

Unfortunately, chips have never been reported to fall with the fish.

Cormorant

CORMORANT FISHING

To this day in China, some fishermen tie light line around the neck of a cormorant—a diving, fish-eating bird. The bird swims underwater and catches a fish. The bird is then retrieved by pulling the line in hand over hand. The leash line prevents the cormorant from swallowing the fish, which is removed from the bird's throat. The same process was used in Peru in the 5th century.

Whitefish

THIS IS THE MOST ABUNDANT GROUP OF FISH IN NORTHERN ALASKA. WHILE NOT OFTEN CONSIDERED A SPORT FISH, THEY ARE USED FOR SUBSISTENCE, BEING TAKEN BY NATIVES FOR THE TABLE AND FOR DOG FOOD. THE SUBTYPES VARY ONLY BY HABITAT PREFERENCES AND SIZE. ALL ARE EXCELLENT AS TABLE FISH.

Smoked whitefish

A traditional fisherman using cormorant birds to catch fish in the Guangxi region of China.

FISHY QUOTES

✦ *"There is more to fishing than catching fish."*
Dame Juliana Berners

✦ *"Once an angler, always a fisherman. If we cannot have the best, we will take the least, and fish for minnows if nothing better is to be had."*
Theodore Gordon

✦ *"Catching fish is as incidental to fishing as making babies is to sex."*
William Humphrey

✦ *"I have fished through fishless days that I remember happily and without regret."*
Roderick Haig-Brown

✦ *"Only those become weary of angling that bring nothing to it but the idea of catching fish."* Rafael Sabatini

✦ *"This planet is covered with sordid men who demand that he who spends time fishing shall show returns in fish."*
Leonidas Hubbard, Jr.

Early Accounts of Angling

★ *On the Nature of Animals*, an account attributed to the ancient Roman commentator Claudius Aelianus, written around the end of the 2nd century C.E., describes Macedonian people fishing in a way that would be an apt description of modern fly fishing.

★ The "Colloquy of Aelfric," dating from around the end of the 10th century, was written in Anglo-Saxon and Latin. It is a manual on taking fish for profit.

★ The 15th-century "Treatyse of Fysshynge Wyth an Angle" by Dame Juliana Berners is illustrated and clearly shows an angler using a rod, line, and float. The work describes how to make tackle as well as how to use bait, hooks, floats, lines, and rods. The text is written by an angler for instructing other anglers.

An illustration from Dame Juliana Berners' 15th-century treatise on fishing, showing a fisherman using a rod and line with a float.

A 2nd-century Roman mosaic from the Villa of the Nile at Leptis Magna in Libya, Africa. The fishermen are using rods and a landing net, and the man on the right is baiting his line.

Excerpt from *On the Nature of Animals*

"I have heard of a Macedonian way of catching fish…These fish feed upon a fly peculiar to the country, which hovers on the river…When then the fish observes a fly on the surface, it swims quietly up, afraid to stir the water above, lest it should scare away its prey; then coming up by its shadow, it opens its mouth gently and gulps down the fly, like a wolf carrying off a sheep…Now though the fishermen know this, they do not use these flies at all for bait for fish…They fasten red (crimson red) wool around a hook, and fix onto the wool two feathers which grow under a cock's wattles, and which in colour are like wax…Their rod is six feet long, and their line is the same length. Then they throw their snare, and the fish, attracted and maddened by the color, comes straight at it, thinking from the pretty sight to gain a dainty mouthful; when, however, it opens its jaws, it is caught by the hook, and enjoys a bitter repast, a captive."

This translation is from William Radcliffe's *Fishing from the Earliest Times* (1921).

Diverse Catfish Facts

Catfish are diverse and, according to a Cornel University study, rank second in total diversity among vertebrates (after skinks). How diverse are catfish? Think of it this way—one in every 10 species of fish and one in every 20 vertebrates is a catfish. That is a lot of catfish. Catfish are found on every continent except the Antarctic. They are found, for the most part, in fresh water. A few species make their homes in salt water.

✦ **Appearance:** Catfish are naked; they have no scales. Some have bony plates, but all are smooth-skinned. They are also toothless and drab-colored, except for the madtoms of North American streams.

✦ **Sensory organs:** The sensory organs of catfish are better developed than in many other types of fish. Most other fish can detect vibrations in the 20 to 1,000 cycles per second range. Catfish hear sounds up to 13,000 cycles per second. Catfish also have at least 250,000 external tastebuds covering their smooth skin. Finally, the back of the catfish's eyes is lined with a layer of crystals that reflect light and provide excellent vision.

✦ **Breeding habits:** Catfish breed in the spring and early summer when the water reaches 70°F (21°C). Males select a spot and females deposit their eggs, which are then fertilized by the male. Shady areas are preferred for nesting. The males, not the females, guard the nest until the eggs hatch and the hatchlings begin to swim and find hiding spots among the vegetation. Spawning occurs at age three or four and once per year.

Brown bullhead catfish

Catfish use their barbels (whiskers) to sense food.

BEST PLACES TO FIND CATFISH

A wels catfish caught in a lake.

* **Streams:** Some stream structures concentrate catfish. Riffles at the head of a pool, the outer edge of a bend, deep water, and undercut banks are all likely to hold fish.

* **Lakes:** Once summer arrives, most lakes will stratify into layers. The lowest layer—10 to 15 feet (3 to 4.6 meters) below the surface and deeper—will have no oxygen and, therefore, no fish, so anglers should fish higher in the water column. Incoming streams concentrate fish because this is where you will most likely find wood, rocks, and drop-offs.

Winter Catfishing

Because the winter food level is low, catfish are on the prowl to find food. What is most available to them is dead fish. Minnows, insect larvae, or cut bait fished near the bottom are best. Do not move the bait. After all, the fish's "natural" food would not be moving. Let the catfish find the bait by its sensitive sense of smell.

FISHY QUOTES

✦ *"The gods do not deduct from man's allotted span the hours spent in fishing."* Babylonian proverb

✦ *"When the Creator made all things, He first made the fishes in the Big Water."* Native American legend

✦ *"May the holes in your net be no larger than the fish in it."* Irish blessing

✦ *"It is not a fish until it is on the bank."* Irish proverb

✦ *"Time is but the streams I go a fishing in. Its thin currents slide away, but eternity remains."* Henry David Thoreau

✦ *"In the morning be first up, and in the evening last to go to bed, for they that sleep catch no fish."* English proverb

Dry Fly Champions (and One Heretic)

In the 19th century, many fly fishermen considered dry fly fishing to be the only proper method. This attitude lives on, unfortunately, and those who embrace it are missing out on many fly-fishing pleasures.

Dry fly

DRY FLY INVENTOR?

It is unclear who developed flies intended to float upon the water, although British tackle dealer James Ogden claimed that he used floating flies in the 1840s.

FIRST WRITTEN MENTION OF DRY FLY FISHING

✦ The December 17th, 1853, issue of the British publication *The Field* contains the first mention of dry fly fishing.

✦ Authored by "The Hampshire Fly Fisher," the article says, "On the other hand, as far as fly fishing is concerned, fishing upstream, unless you are trying the Carshalton dodge and fishing with a dry fly, is very awkward."

✦ The specific mention of the dry fly suggests that these were readily available, and other advertisements promote dry flies with upright wings as early as 1854.

DRY FLY ADVOCATE

✦ After a chance meeting, **Frederic Halford** became a lifelong friend of fellow Englishman George Selwyn Marryat. Marryat, an accomplished angler and fly tyer, taught Halford how to tie and fish the dry fly.

✦ Halford was encouraged to research and write a seminal book on dry fly fishing. Halford wanted Marryat to be his co-author, but Marryat preferred to remain out of the limelight. *Floating Flies and How to Dress Them* (1886) was the first of its kind and established Halford's fame.

✦ Halford's second book, *Dry Fly Fishing in Theory and Practice* (1889), further contributed to his stature as a dry fly fishing advocate. He went on to publish four more books.

PEN NAME

Halford wrote in "The Field" magazine under the pen name "Detached Badger."

FATHER OF AMERICAN DRY FLY FISHING

✦ **Theodore Gordon:** In the late 19th and early 20th centuries, American angler Theodore Gordon wrote a few articles on dry fly fishing for the *Fishing Gazette* and *Forest and Stream* magazines. He fished the Catskill region of New York State. His major contribution to American dry fly fishing was altering existing British flies to better imitate aquatic insects found in America. He was a secretive man and resisted showing his tying techniques to other fly tyers, yet he was given the title "Father of American Dry Fly Fishing" in 1949 by American writer Alfred W. Miller.

✦ **Louis John Rhead:** Perhaps a stronger claim than Theodore Gordon to the title "Father of American Dry Fly Fishing" could be made for Louis Rhead. This British-born American angler started his professional life as an illustrator and gained world recognition as an artist creating posters. In addition, he illustrated classic books such as *Heidi*, *Robin Hood*, *Kidnapped*, *Swiss Family Robinson*, and *The Deerslayer*. Rhead also wrote *American Trout-Stream Insects* (1916), the most comprehensive book on stream insects ever published. In this way, Rhead shared his love of fly fishing.

DRY FLY PURIST

George M. LaBranche was the English author of the classic *The Dry Fly in Fast Water* (1914). He is known for his insistence on presentation as being the most important aspect of successful angling as well as for being a dry fly purist, eschewing any other form of fly fishing.

WET FLY PIONEER

G.E.M. Skues discovered something previously unnoticed by anglers—fish feed mostly on underwater aquatic insects. Anglers who imitated these forms with their flies would be more effective. Pretty simple fact—no? He went on to publish two books on the topic, *Minor Tactics of the Chalk Stream* (1910) and *The Way of a Trout with the Fly and Some Further Studies in Minor Tactics* (1921). His observations and writings created a controversy that lasted his lifetime. The use of dry flies was thought to be the only proper method for fly fishing. Skues's work called into question the popularly held opinion of the day, causing him to be hailed by some as a hero and condemned by others as a heretic.

Wet fly

Farmed tilapia

TILAPIA: FISH AND RICE COMBINATION

- Due to its sweet, mild flesh, tilapia is the third most commercially farmed species of fish worldwide, following carp and salmon. Annual production is more than 1.5 million tons. Africa was this fish's original home, but it is now found around the globe, having been introduced intentionally and unintentionally.
- Tilapia are easy and profitable to raise because they do not require protein in their diet and they are resistant to crowded conditions. These fish show no discrimination as far as where they live. They can be found in lakes, ponds, rivers, streams, and canals.
- An unusual farming method involves planting tilapia and rice at the same time, in the same flooded field. By the time the rice is ready for harvesting, the tilapia will have grown to 6 inches (15 cm) and be ready for market.
- Tilapia average 3 to 4 pounds (1.4 to 1.8 kg) but a 10-pounder (4.5 kg) was caught in Florida. Exotic bait, such as pieces of hot dogs, bread balls, and dog food, can be used to catch them.

MOUTHBROODERS

* Some species of fish protect their eggs by holding them in their mouths until the hatchlings are old enough to fend for themselves. Depending on the species, sometimes the mother takes the eggs, sometimes the father, and sometimes the parents share joint custody.
* Tilapia males, for example, build a nest using their mouth and fins, then swim over to any passing female and lead her back to the nest. The female lays her eggs, which are then fertilized by the male. Immediately, the female takes the eggs into her mouth and leaves. The male remains near the nest, waiting for the next female to swim by, and the process is repeated until the male is exhausted (I should say so). Does the mother ever eat her young? We don't know because her lips are sealed.

Mouthbrooding tilapia

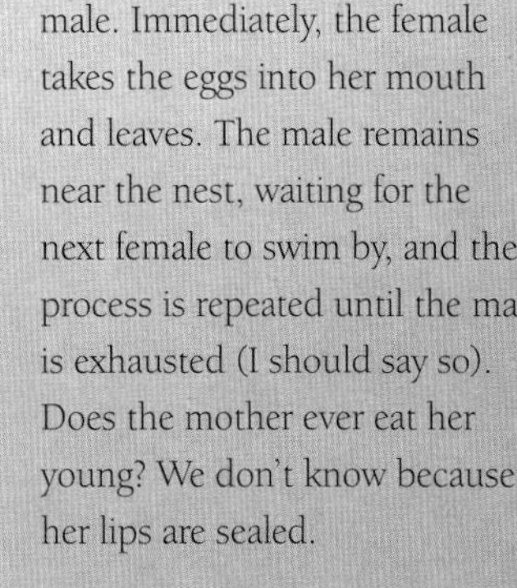

ST. PETER'S FISH

Tilapia are known as St. Peter's fish because of a story in the Bible. In the Gospel of Matthew, Jesus sends the apostle Peter to catch a fish, telling him that he will find a coin in the fish's mouth with which to pay their temple taxes. Tilapia is often identified as the species of fish, although it is not actually named in the Bible.

Statue of St. Peter and a fish at Capernaum, Israel.

Fishing Floats

Made of plastic, feather quill, or reed, fishing floats (also known as bobbers) are attached to the fishing line above the bait. Floats are used to suspend the bait at the required depth, and also act as bite indicators. There are numerous different types of float. Here are a few:

+ **Stick float:** This slim float is attached to the line at the top and bottom of the float, and is generally used in rivers and streams.

+ **Domed-top stick float:** This has a wider top, making it easier to see at greater distances. The importance should be as obvious as the float.

+ **Waggler:** A waggler is a stick-shaped float that is attached to the line at only one end. It is used to fish in still water, and is named for its waggling movement when a fish takes the bait. Wagglers are made in various weights and lengths to match the angler's needs. Many anglers keep a wide variety to better match conditions; some anglers carry too many wagglers.

+ **Marker float:** This is used to provide an indication of where the angler wishes to concentrate his or her efforts. The marker float is cast with a spare rod and held in place by a heavy weight.

A few fishing floats—the range of floats available is vast.

RAINBOW RELATIVES

The rainbow trout and its relatives are among the most important species of sport fish.

✦ **Rainbow trout:** Rainbows are a fast-water fish that live from six to ten years. Prized for their color, they willingly take a fly and are jumpers when hooked. They have been successfully transplanted around the world.

✦ **Steelhead:** Steelhead are the sea-going form of the rainbow trout. Steelhead start in fresh water, then migrate out to sea and remain there for three or four years to fatten and mature. Finally, they return to fresh water to reproduce in the same streams where they were born. They stage off the mouths of rivers until a spring freshet brings them into the river for spawning. Steelhead are among the hardest fighting of the trout family. Spawning runs may be miles long or much shorter, depending on the river receiving the steelhead.

✦ **Cutthroat trout:** The cutthroat trout is named for the distinctive streak of red under its lower jaw. It was first described by Clark during the famous Lewis and Clark expedition across the United States (1804–06) and is named for him (*Oncorhynchus clarkii*). Cutthroat are native to the western United States and Canada. They are easy to catch and make excellent table fare. Those found in coastal rivers migrate to the ocean, where they fatten up for two years before returning to spawn. The primary diet for cutthroat is smaller baitfish, yet scientists are at a loss to explain why worms are such effective bait for this trout.

FISHY QUOTES

- "Wherever the trout are, it's beautiful." Tomas Masaryk

- "They say you forget your troubles on a trout stream, but that's not quite it. What happens is that you begin to see where your troubles fit into the grand scheme of things, and suddenly they're just not such a big deal anymore." John Gierach

- "The true trout fisherman is like a drug addict; he dwells in a tight little dream world all his own, and the men about him, whom he observes obliviously spending their days pursuing money and power, genuinely puzzle him, as he doubtless does them." Robert Traver

- "Often, I've been exhausted on trout streams, uncomfortable, wet, cold, briar-scarred, sunburned, mosquito-bitten, but never, with a flyrod in my hand, have I been unhappy." Charles Kuralt

- "That one does not fish for trout [in England] with spinning lures or with live bait is taken for granted, along with toilet training." William Humphrey

Tickling a rainbow trout.

Tickling Trout

This is a poacher's trick, requiring neither net nor rod nor any other incriminating evidence. The poacher slides a hand where a trout may be hiding. If a fish is found, the poacher lightly tickles the trout's belly and the fish goes into a trance-like state, allowing the poacher to lift the fish out of the water and into a pocket.

Trout Binning

THIS POSSIBLY FICTIONAL METHOD IS DESCRIBED IN AN ENGLISH PERIODICAL OF 1828 THUS: "A MAN WADES ANY ROCKY STREAM WITH A SLEDGE-HAMMER, WITH WHICH HE STRIKES EVERY STONE LIKELY TO CONTAIN FISH. THE FORCE OF THE BLOW STUNS THE FISH, AND THEY ROLL FROM UNDER THE ROCK HALF DEAD, WHEN THE 'BINNER' THROWS THEM OUT WITH HIS HAND." TRUTH IS OFTEN STRANGER THAN FICTION.

Sharks: Weirdness Personified

Sharks were swimming in the oceans 100 million years before the age of the dinosaurs. In 350 million years, sharks have not changed. They are as weird now as they were then, but as the saying goes, if it ain't broke, don't fix it.

+ **Goblin shark:** The goblin shark is believed to be the most primitive shark. It has soft, flabby, pinkish gray skin, and a protruding blade-like proboscis. It is well suited to life in the ocean depths, because it can create a strong vacuum capable of sucking up its prey.

+ **Megamouth shark:** Only 14 specimens have been seen, the first in 1976 near Oahu, Hawaii. It is named for its bathtub-sized mouth, but unlike most other sharks, the 15-foot (4.6-meter) megamouth is a filter feeder.

+ **Cookiecutter shark:** Originally called the cigar shark, this 12- to 17-inch (30- to 43-cm) thin-bodied fish feeds by removing plugs of flesh from larger creatures. It does so through treachery. When a likely predator approaches what appears to be a prey animal, the cookiecutter switches the tables and the predator becomes the prey. Not someone you would like to invite to lunch.

+ **Bigeye thresher shark:** With a vertical height of 4 inches (10 cm), this shark's eyes are proportionately the largest eyes of any non-avian vertebrate. The eyes are like upside-down pears, with the wider part sitting toward the top of the head. This marks it as a predator that strikes from below. At the other end of this fish is a long upper tail fin that it uses to hit and stun its prey.

Sea Dogs

Sharks were known to sailors as sea dogs until the 1500s. The word "shark" probably comes from the Mayan word "xok" (pronounced "shok"). It first appeared after naval admiral Sir John Hawkins took a shark to London in 1569 and told of the large sharks he had seen in the Caribbean Sea.

The bigeye thresher shark—weird at both ends.

A still from the first video footage taken of a frilled shark in its natural haibitat.

```
08-26-04        10:47:18
DEPTH     TEMP     SALIN
2866FT    04.3C    35.0
```

A school of hammerhead sharks in the Galapagos.

Hammerhead shark: Found worldwide, hammerhead sharks usually swim in schools, unlike most other sharks. The unusual head shape, called a cephalofoil, evolved to boost its vision. With an eye positioned at each end of the cephalofoil, they can see 360 degrees in a vertical plane. They are aggressive and have been known to eat their own young.

Frilled shark: This eel-like fish has the head of a lizard and a long, thin body. Its name comes from its many pairs of ruffled gills. It has long jaws alongside the head (rather than under as in other sharks). Most live in Japanese marine waters at depths of 400 to 4,000 feet (120 to 1,220 meters). Rather than swimming like an eel to capture prey, it is believed that the frilled shark strikes as would a snake.

Lanternsharks: These are abundant at depths of 650 to 2,500 feet (200 to 760 meters) from the western Mediterranean through the eastern North Atlantic, and from subarctic Norway to tropical Gabon. Among its subspecies are the dwarf lanternshark, which at 7 inches (18 cm) is thought to be the smallest of all the sharks. The green lanternsharks, found in the Gulf of Mexico, hunt in packs. This allows them to attack prey many times larger than themselves. A study of Japanese brown lanternsharks found 23 percent to be hermaphrodites. As a result, mating can occur whenever two consenting adults meet.

Processed Baits

This type of bait includes table and processed foods that would not usually be part of a fish's natural diet.

Pieces of bread can be put on the hook or turned into a paste.

PASTE BAITS

These high-protein baits are made from ingredients such as bread, cheese, meat, and soy flour mixed with colorings and flavorings. The paste can be molded around the hook.

BOILIES

These are made by adding egg to a marble-sized paste bait and then boiling the mixture. The resulting hard skin prevents smaller fish from eating it. A pop-up boilie is a boilie that has been microwaved to make it buoyant. Commercially produced shelf-life boilies contain food preservatives, and are banned on some waters. Boilies were originally developed for carp fishing, but are now popular for other species as well.

A piece of paste bait molded onto a fishing hook before casting.

LUNCHEON MEAT

An easily obtained bait, luncheon meats are used as is, fried, or flavored to attract tench, chub, carp, and barbel. The meat holds well on a hook—and goes well with mustard on rye bread for the angler as well.

Sweetcorn is one of many table foods that are also effective for fishing. The corn can be dyed or flavored to taste with butter and salt.

Particle Baits

THIS IS THE COLLECTIVE TERM FOR SMALL BAITS, OFTEN USED IN GREAT VOLUMES, SUCH AS BEANS, PEAS, HEMP SEED, AND SWEETCORN. NATURAL BAITS SUCH AS MAGGOTS AND CASTERS ARE ALSO PARTICLE BAITS.

DOG BISCUITS

Some species of fish prefer a floating bait. Dog biscuits work well, and they can also be crushed and added to a paste bait—although the dogs prefer them au naturel.

Marshmallows

These are commonly used as floating bait for carp. If success is lacking, the angler still has an available treat at hand.

A Few Fishing Boats

At one extreme of the fishing boat continuum is the high-powered bass boat. At the other is the slow-going kayak. In between, there is plenty of choice at whatever speed you wish.

JOHNBOAT

The johnboat (or jon boat) is a flat-bottomed, lightweight boat, often made of aluminum. It is low in cost and stable on slowly moving waters. There is no female joanboat version.

DRIFT BOAT

Also known as a McKenzie River dory, this is a specialized 14- to 18-foot (4.3- to 5.5-meter) watercraft with a steeply upturned bow and stern. This craft is desirable because the river's current glides under the flat bottom of the boat, allowing the oarsman to hold the boat steady and give the angler extra time to make a cast.

BELLY BOAT

Also known as a float tube or kick boat, this personal watercraft is usually made of a truck tire inner tube covered by a nylon seat. The angler sits in the seat with his or her legs in the water to provide propulsion. The advantage of the belly boat is its light weight, which allows it to be carried into ponds where larger boats cannot gain access. The name comes from the fact that the angler is sitting in the water up to his or her belly.

Drift Sock

Also known as a drift anchor, this is used to control a boat in rough water. Shaped like a wind sock, it is thrown overboard to act as a floating anchor, slowing down the drift.

Belly boat

Kayak...

BASS BOAT

Holmes Thurmond from Texas is credited with building the first boat dedicated to bass fishing in 1948. His motivation was to build a boat with sloped sides rather than a flat bottom because the wind pushes flat-bottomed boats too easily. In cross-section, Thurmond's boat bottom was wider than the sides. The result was a very stable craft, with plenty of inside storage for tackle. With its sharp bow, it was nicknamed the mosquito or skeeter, with Skeeter becoming the commercial name for this craft.

KAYAK

In recent years, the kayak has become a bona fide fishing watercraft for both fresh and salt water. Some specialists use them for species as large as striped bass. Any time the fish weighs more than the boat, a modern-day version of the Nantucket sleigh ride is sure to follow. When the angler is being towed around by an active fish, the outcome is never certain. A specific advantage of the fishing kayak is its ability to float in very shallow water, allowing the kayak angler to get into places where bigger boats cannot go. Unlike the earliest fishing kayaks, modern designs allow the angler to stand without rolling over. Along the coast of South Africa, fish as large as marlin and sailfish are being taken by unstable kayak anglers.

...Bass boat (just kidding)

Spinning reel

INVENTION OF THE SPINNING REEL

* In 1905, British angler Alfred Holden Illingworth designed the first patented spinning reel. His device was an improvement over the previous practice of hand-winding line around stationary items as a means of storing line between casts.

* His invention involved a mechanical arm that wrapped the line around a fixed spool. The weight of the hook and sinkers caused the line to be pulled from the reel, and the reel did not revolve when a cast was made. This was seen as an improvement, because the spinning reel eliminated the dreaded backlash—a tangle of line caused by a bait-casting spool overrunning, sometimes known as a professional overrun.

* Spinning reels also allowed the use of lighter lures, because the fixed spool of the spinning reel did not have to overcome the inertia of the casting reel's spool. Illingworth's reel was handheld, and later improvements led to a reel that could be mounted on the fishing rod.

Nest Protectors

IN SPECIES SUCH AS CATFISH AND BASS, THE FEMALES LAY THEIR EGGS AND THEN LEAVE TOWN. THE MALE STAYS TO GUARD THE NEST AND HATCHLINGS. AS THE YOUNG FISH GROW, SOME BECOME ADEPT AT HIDING IN THE WEEDS. SOME DO NOT. SOME GET EATEN BY DEAR OLD DAD.

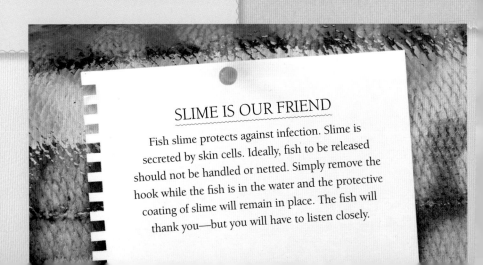

SLIME IS OUR FRIEND

Fish slime protects against infection. Slime is secreted by skin cells. Ideally, fish to be released should not be handled or netted. Simply remove the hook while the fish is in the water and the protective coating of slime will remain in place. The fish will thank you—but you will have to listen closely.

Bluegill

BLUEGILL: SCRAPPY FIGHTERS

★ This member of the sunfish family is caught all over the world, and is prized for its scrappy fighting and delicious, flaky, sweet meat.

★ Bluegill are also known as bream, brim, blue perch, blue sunfish, copperbelly, bluebream, red-breasted bream, bluegill sunfish, and roach. The variety of names speaks to the wide popularity of this little fish.

★ Coloration varies by location, and they may be olive, dark blue, purple, yellow, or green, depending on the water they call home.

★ Big bluegills average 1 to 3 pounds (0.45 to 1.4 kg), but the IGFA world record is 4 pounds 12 ounces (2.15 kg). These fish grow 1 to 4 inches (2.5 to 10 cm) per year, depending on the water temperature. Unlike many other fish, the males are larger than the females.

★ Every other sport fish feeds on bluegills. To survive, each female lays 40,000 eggs, which are guarded by the males. Bluegills feed mostly on insects, crayfish, fish eggs, snails, minnows, and worms.

Vicarious Angling

The assortment of television fishing shows continues to grow. Every type of fishing has a program, or two, or eighteen, devoted to its piscatorial preference. One thing they have in common is that whenever anyone catches anything, someone will say, "That's a nice fish." This is repeated over and over and over ad infinitum, until it is too much to bear and the viewer is forced to watch with the sound turned off. The only thing worse is the fish kissing that takes place. Apparently, this started several years ago, when a bass-fishing host began kissing his fish in an act of appreciation. Unbelievably, this caught on and hosts are now smooching fish from dawn to dusk. It gags me just to think about it.

Pucker up!

American shad

Shad

The shad lives mostly at sea except for spawning, when it runs up rivers. Shad die after spawning. They do not build nests, but instead broadcast their eggs, which drift for three days. After nine months, the 4-inch (10-cm) shad leave the river for the sea, where they grow to 30 inches (76 cm). Fly fishing has become a popular means of catching American shad. They are known as the poor man's salmon in tribute to their fighting ability. Most shad are smoked for the table and shad roe is excellent.

Ghillie

From the Scottish Gaelic dialect "gille," meaning lad or servant, ghillie is the name for a person who looks after an angler and shows him or her where to fish—in other words, a fishing guide.

An illustration of shad fishing featured in a Parisian magazine in 1860. Shad were traditionally caught along with salmon in nets.

Salmon planked and ready for cooking. Shad—poor man's salmon—can be prepared by the same method, but it is recommended that the fish be thrown in the fire and the boards eaten.

THE PROOF OF THE PUDDING IS IN THE EATING

Any cookbook will describe poaching, baking, and frying. Cooking over a campfire, however, allows for a unique, little-known method called planking.

1) Dress the fish and cut nearly through from stomach to back along the entire length of the fish. Do not cut completely through. The skin should remain intact.

2) Unfold the fish and tack it to a well-soaked cedar board, skin side against the board.

3) Rub the fish with the following mixture:
   - 1 tablespoon brown sugar
   - 1 tablespoon salt
   - 2 teaspoons ancho chili powder
   - 1 teaspoon ground cumin
   - ½ teaspoon black pepper

4) Prop the board close to a bed of hot coals.

5) When the flesh flakes easily, it is done.

FISHY QUOTES

✦ *"Salmon in Britain is poached… in milk. The taste is describable. Poached milk."* William Humphrey

✦ *"Our tradition is that of the first man who sneaked away to the creek when the tribe did not really need fish."* Roderick Haig-Brown

✦ *"Fishing has a reputation as an innocuous, fairly mindless pastime enjoyed mostly by shiftless people."* Paul Schullery

✦ *"At the outset, the fact should be recognized that the community of fishermen constitute a separate class or subrace among the inhabitants of the earth."* Grover Cleveland

✦ *"If fishing interferes with your business, give up your business."* Sparse Grey Hackle

ICE FISHING

You really have to want to fish if you are an ice angler. Ice fishing combines the best—and worst—of fishing with survival skills. The equipment carried by ice anglers is uniquely adapted to fishing through frozen water.

※ A sled makes getting on and off the ice easier. There is too much gear to expect to carry it by hand, and the warm clothing required cuts down on the weight that can be carried.

※ Some implement is required to make holes—something not necessary during sane angling seasons. An ice chisel or ax may do the trick. However, if the ice is 3 feet (90 cm) thick or more, a gas-powered ice auger is the preferred method for drilling holes. You can pay for the cost of a new auger in one day by renting it out to anglers already exhausted by trying to make holes by hand.

※ A skimmer will keep the holes from refreezing during the outing. The skimmer looks like a slotted metal spoon. Be advised that if you pick it up in your bare hand, it will freeze to your skin. Are we having fun yet?

※ Without an ice house, you will need all the clothes you own and half of what you can borrow if staying alive is of the slightest importance to you.

※ Fishing devices include a jigging rod (a small rod that the angler jerks, or jigs, occasionally), a tip-up or ice trap (a device with an underwater spool that trips a flag, indicating that a fish has taken the bait), and in some places a spear.

※ An assortment of lures and/or bait can be used. Minnows or wax worms also work well. Some anglers keep the worms in their mouth to prevent them from freezing. I cannot recommend this, but you can take your chances.

※ Diehard ice anglers also bring brandy by the barrel. They end up happy even if no fish are caught.

Ice auger and jigging rod

Skimmer

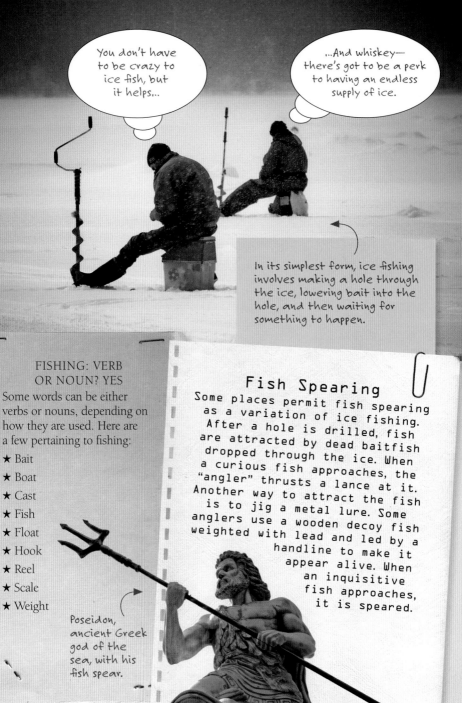

You don't have to be crazy to ice fish, but it helps...

...And whiskey—there's got to be a perk to having an endless supply of ice.

In its simplest form, ice fishing involves making a hole through the ice, lowering bait into the hole, and then waiting for something to happen.

FISHING: VERB OR NOUN? YES

Some words can be either verbs or nouns, depending on how they are used. Here are a few pertaining to fishing:

★ Bait
★ Boat
★ Cast
★ Fish
★ Float
★ Hook
★ Reel
★ Scale
★ Weight

Poseidon, ancient Greek god of the sea, with his fish spear.

Fish Spearing

Some places permit fish spearing as a variation of ice fishing. After a hole is drilled, fish are attracted by dead baitfish dropped through the ice. When a curious fish approaches, the "angler" thrusts a lance at it. Another way to attract the fish is to jig a metal lure. Some anglers use a wooden decoy fish weighted with lead and led by a handline to make it appear alive. When an inquisitive fish approaches, it is speared.

Izaak Walton

Englishman Izaak Walton (1593–1683) is widely regarded as the most important of the early angling writers. His *Compleat Angler* (1653) is often quoted—three extracts are provided below. Walton was a skilled angler and his work celebrates the theme that fishing is an art that transcends catching fish.

Fishing in style for the lady angler.

+ **On the use of a landing net:** "But what say you now? There is a trout now and a good one too, if I can but hold him; and two or three more turns will tire him. Now you see he lies still, and the sleight is to land him: reach me that landing-net. So, Sir, now he is mine own: what say you now, is not this worth all my labour and your patience."

+ **On the benefit of a fish diet:** "The casting off of Lent and other fish days, which hath not only given the lie to so many learned, pious wise founders of colleges, for which we should be ashamed, hath doubtless been the chief cause of those many putrid, shaking, intermittent agues, unto which this nation of ours is now more subject, than those wiser countries that feed on herbs and plenty of fish."

+ **On the use of a reel:** During Walton's time, reels were just beginning to come into use and his description leaves something to be desired. His first edition did not mention the reel at all. Not until the second edition did Walton write about them: "Note also, that many used to fish for Salmon with a ring or wire on the top of their rod, through which the line may run to as great a length as is needful, when he is hooked. And to that end, some use a wheel about the middle of their rod, or near the hand, which is to be observed better by seeing one of them than by a large demonstration of words."

FISHING TACKLE IN THE 1600s

The popularity of angling during Izaak Walton's time can be understood by the fact that the 1650s marked the start of the tackle manufacturing trade. English writer Gervase Markham advised anglers not to bother making their own rods because they could be bought in almost any haberdashery ("Country Contentments," 1631). Thus, a gentleman could buy both clothing and fishing equipment in a men's shop. Women, apparently, were on their own.

HISTORY OF THE PLASTIC WORM

* The first patent for a plastic worm type of bait was granted in the United States in 1877. The lure was made of rubber, but it did not perform swimmingly.

* In 1949, Nick Crème, from Akron, Ohio, poured vinyl into homemade molds. He also experimented by scenting the worms with—what else?—ground-up live worms.

* In 1969, Tom Mann, from Lake Eufaula, Alabama, developed a soft worm in translucent colors and artificial scents that were part of the plastic blending process rather than additives.

* In 1972, the Mister Twister company created a flat, curly tail that fluttered when retrieved, even at the slowest speed. About this same time, bass-fishing tournaments exposed more and more anglers to a variety of plastic worms. This exposure created a great demand for new, innovative plastic worms and lures.

* Today, there are nearly 90 plastic worm manufacturers in the United States alone. Contemporary bass anglers seldom set out without hundreds of these baits in various sizes, colors, and scents.

Dr. James Henshall

Henshall's *Book of the Black Bass* (1881) was written from an angler's perspective and was intended to be instructional. Responsible for turning attention from trout to bass, Henshall is considered to be the father of bass fishing in the United States.

The earliest plastic lures were shaped like worms, but there are now also shapes like minnows, grubs, frogs, and crustaceans.

French-fried Worms?

The French fry is a soft plastic worm that is cut to resemble a crinkle-cut French-fried potato. Why? Who knows? The fish aren't talking.

How Many, Exactly?

There are more than 30,000 species of fish and the number keeps growing as more are discovered. The number of known fish species is more than the sum of birds, amphibians, reptiles, and mammals combined.

FISH NAMED FOR COLORS

Finally, a strategy for naming fish that makes sense.

- Black bass
- Bluefin tuna
- Bluefish
- Brown trout
- Goldeneye cichlid
- Golden trout
- Lemon shark
- Olive flounder
- Pink happy
- Pink salmon
- Rainbow trout
- Redfin perch
- White bass
- Whitefish
- Yellow chub
- Yellowfin tuna
- Yellowfish
- Yellow perch

BLUEFISH: PREDATOR AND BATTLER

+ The bluefish is native to both sides of the Atlantic. It is valued for its hard fight when hooked. It has a mouth full of sharp, cone-shaped teeth, capable of chopping through a broom handle—evidence of this fish's predatory nature.

+ Bluefish usually run to 20 pounds (9 kg) and 40 inches (102 cm). The IGFA world record is 31 pounds 12 ounces (14.4 kg).

+ Bluefish are opportunistic and eat virtually any kind of baitfish. Anglers watch for diving birds to show them where the bluefish are actively feeding. Schools of feeding blues will charge through schools of baitfish and drive them up to the surface, where pieces of baitfish are taken by the sea birds. Anglers casting cut bait, floating plugs, or large flies will be rewarded with an immediate strike.

Bluefish

HANDLINING

Handlining may be the simplest form of fishing. No rod or reel is used. The fisherman drifts in a boat with a handheld baited line. The fish bites and the fisherman pulls the line in hand over hand. This may be the source of the saying, "A fisherman is a jerk at one end of a line waiting for a jerk at the other."

Beer Can Fishing

A variation of handlining is beer can (or pop can) fishing. One end of a handline is tied to a beer can and the line is wrapped around the can. The loose end of the line is rigged with a baited hook. Holding the can, the fisherman twirls the weighted line around a few times and then releases it. The line unwinds from the can, casting the baited hook into the water. This version of handlining can be done from shore. Upon feeling a tug, the fisherman responds in kind and a fish is brought to hand. Empty beer cans work best—and there is usually no shortage of them.

The Old Man and the Sea

+ Published in 1952, this short novel was the last fiction written and published by Ernest Hemingway in his lifetime. The protagonist, Santiago, is an aging handlining fisherman who struggles with a giant marlin but loses it to sharks.

+ The book won the Pulitzer Prize in 1953, and was cited when Hemingway was awarded the Nobel Prize in Literature in 1954.

+ The 1958 movie based on the novel won the Academy Award for best original score. The movie also received nominations for best color cinematography and best actor for its star, Spencer Tracy. The budget ran far over because they could not find a marlin of sufficient size to match Hemingway's description in the book.

FISHY QUOTES

+ "Somebody just back of you while you are fishing is as bad as someone looking over your shoulder while you write a letter to your girl." Ernest Hemingway

+ "Creeps and idiots cannot conceal themselves for long on a fishing trip." John Gierach

+ "Most fishermen swiftly learn that it's a pretty good rule never to show a favorite spot to any fisherman you wouldn't trust with your wife!" John Voelker

+ "Regardless of what you think about our penal system, the fact is that every man in jail is one less potential fisherman to clutter up your favorite pool or pond." Ed Zern

Ernest Hemingway (on right in striped sweater) with a record-breaking 468-pound (212-kg) black marlin that he caught off the coast of Cuba, c. 1935.

Three dorsal fins

Two anal fins

ATLANTIC COD: EASILY DISTINGUISHED SHAPE

+ Native to most of the North Atlantic, the Atlantic cod is characterized by its three dorsal fins and two anal fins.

+ Inshore cod average 30 inches (76 cm) and 6 to 12 pounds (2.7 to 5.4 kg). Offshore cod are 40 inches (102 cm) and 25 pounds (11.3 kg). The cod is a popular offshore sport fish and many anglers fish for them from party boats.

+ Atlantic cod mainly eat small crustaceans but will eat almost anything, including lobsters, sea urchins, crabs, shad, capelin, and mackerel. Strange things found in cod stomachs include rope, shoes, jewelry, and ducks. Go figure.

Crowded Seas

The Blue Sea Sport Angling Club of Malta had 785 anglers registered for a single sea-angling competition—a Guinness record. Imagine the cost for fuel.

No More Fish and Chips?

Invented in the mid-1800s, fish and chips consist of battered, fried fish and deep-fried, slab-cut potatoes. They became popular in Britain and also spread to areas colonized by Britain. Thanks to the development of trawling in the North Sea, abundant fish allowed fish and chips to become a stock meal of the British working classes. Why no more "fish and chips"? The Fish Labeling Regulations of 2003 required that fish must be sold with the specific species named. As a result, you can now purchase "cod and chips" but not "fish and chips."

Cod and chips?

Record Catches (continued from page 50)

- Halibut, Atlantic
  418 lb 13 oz (190 kg)
- Halibut, Pacific
  459 lb 0 oz (208.2 kg)
- Hottentot
  3 lb 12 oz (1.7 kg)
- Ling, European
  88 lb 6 oz (40.1 kg)
- Mackerel, Atlantic
  2 lb 10 oz (1.2 kg)
- Mackerel, king
  93 lb 0 oz (42.18 kg)
- Mahseer
  95 lb 0 oz (43.09 kg)
- Mahseer, golden
  27 lb 0 oz (12.25 kg)
- Marlin, black
  1,560 lb 0 oz
  (707.61 kg)
- Marlin, blue (Atlantic)
  1402 lb 2 oz (636 kg)
- Marlin, blue (Pacific)
  1376 lb 0 oz (624.14 kg)
- Marlin, striped
  494 lb 0 oz (224.1 kg)
- Marlin, white
  181 lb 14 oz (82.5 kg)
- Monkfish, European
  57 lb 4 oz (25.96 kg)
- Muskellunge
  67 lb 8 oz (30.61 kg)
- Perch, European
  6 lb 6 oz (2.9 kg)
- Perch, Nile
  230 lb 0 oz (104.32 kg)

- Perch, yellow
  4 lb 3 oz (1.91 kg)
- Permit
  60 lb 0 oz (27.21 kg)
- Pickerel, chain
  9 lb 6 oz (4.25 kg)
- Pickerel, redfin
  2 lb 4 oz (1.02 kg)
- Pike, northern
  55 lb 1 oz (25 kg)
- Piranha, black
  8 lb 7 oz (3.83 kg)
- Piranha, red
  3 lb 7 oz (1.55 kg)
- Pollack, European
  27 lb 6 oz (12.41 kg)
- Pompano, African
  50 lb 8 oz (22.9 kg)
- Pompano, Florida
  8 lb 4 oz (3.76 kg)
- Prickleback, monkeyface
  3 lb 4 oz (1.47 kg)
- Pumpkinseed
  1 lb 6 oz (0.63 kg)
- Roach
  4 lb 1 oz (1.84 kg)
- Rohu
  27 lb 8 oz (12.5 kg)
- Sailfish, Atlantic
  141 lb 1 oz (64 kg)
- Sailfish, Pacific
  221 lb 0 oz (100.24 kg)
- Salmon, Atlantic
  79 lb 2 oz (35.89 kg)
- Salmon, chinook
  97 lb 4 oz (44.11 kg)

- Salmon, chum
  35 lb 0 oz (15.87 kg)
- Salmon, coho
  33 lb 4 oz (15.08 kg)
- Salmon, pink
  14 lb 13 oz (6.74 kg)
- Salmon, sockeye
  15 lb 3 oz (6.88 kg)
- Sawfish, large-tooth
  890 lb 8 oz (403.92 kg)
- Shad, American
  11 lb 4 oz (5.1 kg)
- Shad, Mediterranean
  1 lb 15 oz (0.88 kg)
- Shark, bull
  697 lb 12 oz (316.5 kg)
- Shark, great white
  2,664 lb 0 oz
  (1,208.38 kg)
- Shark, mako
  1,221 lb 0 oz (553.84 kg)
- Skate
  214 lb 0 oz (97.07 kg)
- Snakehead
  17 lb 4 oz (7.85 kg)
- Snapper, cubera
  124 lb 12 oz (56.59 kg)
- Snapper, grey
  17 lb 0 oz (7.71 kg)
- Snapper, mutton
  30 lb 4 oz (13.72 kg)
- Snapper, red
  50 lb 4 oz (22.79 kg)
- Snapper, yellowtail
  11 lb 0 oz (4.98 kg)

(continued on page 171)

Lipless Crankbait

Also known as vibrating plugs, these produce intense vibrations and are popular in the early season, when the water is cool and fish are looking for prey with a tight rather than a slow wiggle. Their vibrations make them ideal for low light conditions, and some have rattles built in to attract fish by sound as well as sight. They can be fished at any depth and can be retrieved quickly, so an angler can cover a lot of water in search of fish.

A lipless crankbait with a built-in rattle.

Books, Books, Books

In the 1960s, Helena and Douglas Milne donated their collection of fishing books, periodicals, artwork, and ephemera to the University of New Hampshire. Containing more than 3,500 pieces, it is one of the largest collections in the United States.

My brain may be the size of a pea, but I still manage to send anglers home talking to themselves.

FISHING TOMFOOLERY

Anglers have a sense of humor; they must—it is a survival skill. Here are some examples:

* The pike is a large fish found in North America and parts of Europe. The best time to fish for pike is two days before your arrival and two days after your departure.

* A fishing cap is used to trap biting insects, giving them time for leisurely dining.

* The lure that guarantees a record catch is never to be found in your tackle box.

* A digital camera is a failed truth-detecting device, usually found in an angler's wettest pocket.

* How much fishing tackle guarantees a divorce? I don't know, but the experiment is nearly complete.

* There is a fine line between fishing and standing in a river looking like an idiot.

FISHY QUOTES

✦ *"There is nothing more absurd than a fine large man being played by a fish."* Theodore Gordon

✦ *"It has always been my private conviction that any man who pits his intelligence against a fish and loses has it coming."* John Steinbeck

✦ *"There he stands, draped in more equipment than a telephone lineman, trying to outwit an organism with a brain no bigger than a breadcrumb, and getting licked in the process."* Paul O'Neil

✦ *"Only an extraordinary person would purposely risk being outsmarted by a creature often less than 12 inches long—over and over again."* Janna Bialek

Ah, a metal rod. Mind if I use it to do some flossing while you admire my teeth?

Piranha: Misunderstood Terror

Say the word "piranha" and everyone runs screaming from the river. In fact, piranha are timid fish that school together for protection from predators such as caimans, dolphins, and cormorants. Piranha have been described by scientists as "basically like regular fish but with really large teeth." I've seen the videos—I know better.

INVITE A CATFISH TO DINNER

Catfish are an important source of protein around the world. They are valued for their sweet, mild taste. Catfish are inexpensive and easy to raise commercially. In the United States, 46 percent of aquaculture production is accounted for by catfish. In Africa and Asia, walking catfish and shark catfish are heavily cultivated. (Do you think walking catfish are rounded up by tiny riders on seahorseback?)

Types of Hooks

+ Hooks are most often named either for their shape, function, or the geographic region where they originated. Some manufacturers name their hooks for the insects that fly tyers create, such as nymph and caddis.

+ Most hooks originally met standards for wire gauge, shank length, shape of bend, and size of gape. Variations appeared as anglers demanded specialized hooks for specific purposes. For example, a longer (2xl) or shorter (1xs) shank than standard, or heavier (2x heavy) or lighter (3x light) wire.

+ Originally, hooks conformed to standard sizes—for example, a size 7 hook was heavier, longer, and bigger than a size 8. The odd-size hooks were then eliminated, leaving only even sizes. The smallest hook currently in production is the size 32 (about the size of this letter "J"). It is used to imitate the smallest gnats that trout may feed on. The largest hook, size 20/0, is appropriate for 800-pound (363-kg) marlin and is about 6 inches (15 cm) long. Handmade size 27/0 hooks (odd sizes now only appear as really large handmade hooks) are used for 2,000-pound (907-kg) great white sharks. Because they are handmade, the sky is the limit on length, but for a great white shark, the longer, the better.

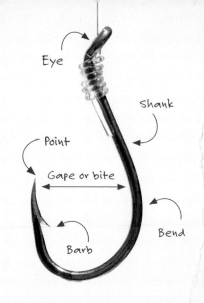

Eye

Shank

Point

Gape or bite

Bend

Barb

Reducing Injury to Fish

+ **Barbless and microbarbed hooks:** Some hooks are made either without barbs or with a smaller barb than regular hooks. This makes it easier to remove the hook without injuring the fish. It also permits bait, such as maggots, to remain alive much longer.

+ **Circle hooks:** Rather than being shaped like a "J," the circle hook is made so that the point is turned perpendicular to the shank. This forms a rough circle or oval shape. When the fish takes the bait, the angler pulls in the slack without jerking the hook. The circle hook then slides into the corner of the fish's mouth. With the circle hook, the fish does not swallow the hook, so it cannot be hooked in the gut or throat and mortality is greatly reduced. Circle-hooked fish also fight harder than gut-hooked fish.

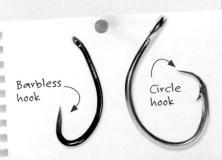

Barbless hook

Circle hook

ELECTRIC EEL

- Ol' Sparky is not an eel but a knifefish and a close relative of the catfish.
- Electric eels live in South America in the fresh waters of the Amazon and Orinoco River basins.
- They are air breathers and must surface every ten minutes.
- The electric eel grows to 6 feet (1.8 meters) and puts out enough amps to kill a person. It uses its charge to hunt and to protect itself.
- The eel's brain sends a signal to electric organ dischargers in the abdomen to produce a charge.
- It can generate 500 volts and one ampere—0.75 amps is enough to do you in. The electric eel can generate charges for over an hour.
- It breeds in the dry season and males make nests from their saliva for females to drop their eggs into.

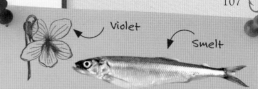

Violet

Smelt

How the Smelt Got Its Name

According to Englishman Thomas Boosey's *Anecdotes of Fish and Fishing* (1887), the smelt derives its name from its having the smell of a violet or fresh cucumber. Hmmmm, I wonder what catfish smells like.

Grunions mating in the sand.

Sand Spawners

Californians are blessed with the grunion and a unique fishing opportunity. Grunion are small fish and members of the smelt family. Grunion leave the water at night to spawn on the beach for four consecutive nights during the new and full moons. As a wave breaks on the beach, grunion swim as far up the slope as possible to complete their spawning run. Hordes of screaming Californians scamper around catching them by hand and filling buckets. There is no "creel" limit, but people are encouraged to take only what they can use as table fare. The fish don't seem to enjoy it as much as the people.

CATFISH FOOD PREFERENCES

Catfish find their food primarily by smell, using the specialized receptor cells in their barbels (whiskers) to help them. The stronger the scent, the better. This is a handy skill, given the fact that they do most of their feeding in the darkness of night. The lesson for anglers? Fish smelly baits after dark.

✦ **Blue catfish:** Although blue catfish feed mostly on other fish, they will eat almost anything. Angling for them suggests shiners or stinkbaits right on the bottom. Blues have a more sophisticated body shape than other catfish, so they are fast enough to feed on both prey fish and insects.

✦ **Channel catfish:** If you offer it, they will come. Being omnivores, like most catfish, they enjoy occasional insect larvae, crayfish, mollusks, crustaceans, fish (dead or alive), and even some fruits and berries. Contrary to popular opinion, channel catfish do not enjoy carrion. Picky, picky, picky.

✦ **Bullhead:** Scavenger is an apt description for this catfish's lack of preferences. It is not particular and seems to be satisfied with the lowest order of food. Brown bullhead eat carrion, worms, and smaller fish. The yellow variety eats snails and sometimes organic decay. This characteristic makes selecting bullhead bait a no-brainer.

✦ **Flathead catfish:** This variety prefers live fish to almost all other baits. It enjoys shiners, chubs, shad, crayfish, bass, and even other catfish. Compared to other catfish, flatheads are predators. They prefer to fish the shallows after dark and are known to fish in gangs—much like sharks, but with nicer personalities.

✦ **White catfish:** The white catfish does not always feed after dark. It also eats fish eggs, insects, and—just for a balanced diet—plants, making its feeding habits different from most other catfish.

Is that a dead fish I smell? It's making my mouth water.

Blue catfish

Fisherman casting a weighted net.

Cast-net Casting

Although technically not a sport-fishing technique, net casting is a way to capture baitfish.

❖ The cast net is first mentioned in Norse mythology. Rán, a sea goddess, cast her fishing net to capture men who went to sea. In ancient Rome, the retiarius gladiator, or net fighter, was armed with a net and trident.

❖ Modern cast nets vary from 4 to 12 feet (1.2 to 3.7 meters), with sport-fishing nets measuring about 4 feet (1.2 meters). The perimeter of the net has weights to carry the net down quickly, trapping baitfish. The net is closed when a handline is pulled, closing the bottom and trapping the baitfish.

❖ Cast nets work best when the depth of the water is no greater than the diameter of the net. Otherwise, the fish have too great an opportunity to escape before the net approaches the bottom.

FISHY QUOTES

✦ *"One of the outstanding peculiarities of angling is its inexplicable capacity to inspire almost unanimous disagreement among its followers."* John Alden Knight

✦ *"Angling may be said to be so like the mathematics, that it can never be fully learnt."* Izaak Walton

✦ *"When, I wonder, are folks going to learn that it is a dangerous thing to attempt to lay down hard and fast rules about fishing?"* John Alden Knight

✦ *"When you find someone who answers all the questions, you can be sure that he doesn't fish enough to know what it's all about or else—well, just or else."* Ray Bergman

✦ *"The aerospace industry requires less technical jargon than the average bass fisherman."* Patrick F. McManus

✦ *"Calling fishing a hobby is like calling brain surgery a job."* Paul Schullery

Do Fish Sleep? Nope

Fish rest but do not sleep like mammals. Fish must keep their gills working to take in oxygen, so instead of hitting the sheets as many mammals do, fish go into a restful stage that allows their gills to continue working.

Some fish have teeth and some do not. As far as I know, none has dentures.

Do Fish Have Teeth?

Plankton feeders, such as the whale shark, do not require teeth. In fish that have teeth, they are shaped like cones, being pointy at one end to capture and hold slippery forage fish. Salmonoids also have teeth on their tongues. Sharks have flat, sharp, serrated teeth designed for slicing. The shark's teeth are modified scales. Other fish, such as the bonefish, have crushers instead of teeth to help them feed on shellfish. None of them requires dental insurance.

Pink salmon

CUBA

MACABI

PESCA DEPORTIVA

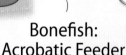

SCUD

Scud, also known as freshwater shrimp, are easy pickings for fish because the scud have limited mobility. For this reason, and because of their abundance, fish feed freely on scud. Fly fishermen make imitations to mimic these food forms.

Bonefish: Acrobatic Feeder

Bonefish are native to the tropical waters around Florida, the Bahamas, and Bermuda. They move into sandy flat shallows to feed on worms, mollusks, shrimp, and crabs. When feeding, they go vertical, standing on their heads with their tails sticking out of the water. Bonefish are prized by anglers for their speed when hooked. The long runs when hooked require reels loaded with at least 600 feet (180 meters) of line.

Scud

VIPERFISH

The viperfish has so many sharp fangs that they all cannot fit inside its mouth. The longest exterior ones curve back toward its eyes. Vipers attack at full speed with open mouths. To protect itself from the furiousness of its attack, the first vertebra behind the head acts like a shock absorber. Otherwise, the fish would knock itself out each time it fed.

ROPING TOOTHY CRITTERS

The gar is a primitive fish that has changed little over eons. It has a long thin body and an extended jaw filled with needle-like teeth. The largest species, the alligator gar, can reach 300 pounds (136 kg) and has two rows of teeth on each side of its upper jaw. Adults will feed on baitfish or waterfowl. No bait is used for catching gar. Instead, a 6-inch (15-cm) frayed nylon rope is used as a hookless lure. The nylon gets caught in the fish's teeth as securely as if it were hooked and the fish cannot get away until released by the angler.

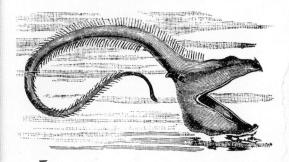

Gulper Eel: Appetite With Fins

THIS EEL IS KNOWN FOR ITS LARGE, HINGED MOUTH THAT IS LARGER THAN ITS BODY, MAKING IT POSSIBLE TO SWALLOW A PREY LARGER THAN ITSELF. BOTH THE LOWER JAW AND THE STOMACH CAN EXTEND TO ACCOMMODATE A LARGE LUNCH.

Alligator gar

TYPES OF TUNA
(THAT MAY END UP IN CANS)

Tuna is an important commercial fish as well as a prized sport fish. Whereas large bluefin tuna are likely to be used for sushi, the species below are generally used as canned tuna or baitfish.

+ **Yellowfin tuna:** The yellowfin is named for the yellow stripe on its sides and fins. Maximum size of the yellowfin is 7 feet (2.1 meters) and 440 pounds (200 kg). This species of tuna prefers warm, tropical/subtropical waters. Fishing for the yellowfin was once done with nets, killing many dolphins in the process.

+ **Bigeye tuna:** The bigeye looks like the yellowfin but, as the name implies, its eyes are very big. Bigeyes are found in tropical and subtropical waters of the Atlantic, Pacific, and Indian oceans. The bigeye reaches 6 feet (1.8 meters) in length and weighs in at 400 pounds (181 kg).

+ **Albacore:** Albacore are found in the Atlantic Ocean, Pacific Ocean, and the Mediterranean Sea. They top out at about 4 feet (1.2 meters) in length and 88 pounds (40 kg). Their distinctive characteristics are exceptionally long pectoral fins. The canned version may be labeled as "white" tuna.

+ **Skipjack tuna:** Skipjacks average 3 feet (90 cm) and 40 pounds (18.1 kg). They prefer to school under floating objects in tropical waters around the world. Identification is simple, because they are the only tuna with four to six stripes running the length of their body.

+ **Little tunny:** The little tunny is the smallest—up to 35 pounds (15.9 kg)—and most common tuna in the Atlantic, found from Brazil to New England as well as in the Mediterranean. It is also known as mackerel tuna, bonito, false albacore, or albie. Unlike other tuna that are valued as table fare, the little tunny is not consumed but, instead, is used as bait for shark and marlin fishing. The little tunny is an inshore fish, making it accessible to sport fishermen, and it is prized because it can rip off line at 40 miles per hour (64 kph). It lives anyplace where baitfish are likely to congregate. Little tunny form large schools, and their feeding is often obvious on the surface, with the baitfish leaping clear of the water as they try to avoid the tunny.

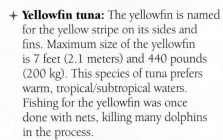

Albacore

Largest Tuna on Rod and Reel

According to the World Records Academy, the 33-year-old Guinness World Record was broken by a 405-pound (183.7-kg) yellowfin tuna caught off San Diego, California, in 2010. It took angler Michael Livingston 160 minutes to bring in his catch.

Commercial fishermen catching yellowfin tuna by pole and line fishing.

SUSTAINABLE TUNA

❖ There is worldwide concern about the non-selective fishing methods that may be used to catch tuna commercially. The most well-known bycatch to capture public attention is the dolphin, but other bycatch species of concern include sharks, rays, turtles, and endangered tuna such as the bigeye.

❖ Commercial longliners and seiners (boats that use large nets for fishing) can no longer take giant tuna. Instead, airplanes are hired to look for fish so that harpoon boats can take the tuna. The hiring is worth the expense because giant tuna are highly sought for the Japanese sushi market and demand high prices.

❖ There is increasing pressure for canned tuna retailers to source tuna caught by line and pole—a sustainable and bycatch-friendly method.

Longline Fishing

This uses a long line with many baited hooks at predetermined distances. The line may extend for many miles and have up to 2,500 baited hooks. Longlines set near the surface catch fish such as swordfish and tuna. Longlines set near the bottom catch cod and halibut.

EELS ON THE MOVE

* American and European eels are wide-ranging fish, found as far north as Greenland and as far south as Brazil. In the United States, eels find their way to New Mexico, reaching there from the Gulf of Mexico via the Rio Grande, and are common throughout the Caribbean.

* Both American and European eels spawn in the winter in the Sargasso Sea, just north of Cuba. Neither eel eggs nor adults have been found in the Sargasso, but newly hatched eels are plentiful. Young eels are transparent and leaf-shaped. Scientists believe that spawning takes place at great depth and the adults then die.

* Adult eels spend their lives in fresh water. American eels enter rivers at three years of age. European eels have a longer migration that may take them up to six years to complete.

* Upon reaching fresh water, female eels migrate as far upstream as possible, swimming into smaller and smaller tributaries. The males, apparently too lazy to join the females, stay close to coastlines and meet up with the females in time for a trip to the Sargasso Sea to spawn.

Heading for a romantic break in the Sargasso Sea.

Curing Alcoholism With an Eel

According to Englishman Thomas Boosey's *Anecdotes of Fish and Fishing* (1887), alcoholism can be cured by placing an eel in a bottle of wine. A week after the eel dies, remove what is left of the eel and offer the wine to an alcoholic. If he survives, he will be cured. The cure may be worse than the disease. What are friends for?

Sort of Live Birth

SOME FISH, SUCH AS SHARKS, RETAIN
FERTILIZED EGGS WITHIN THEIR BODY
AND RELEASE THEM LATER AS LIVE BIRTH.

Apparently, newborn sharks, known
as pups, are cute and cuddly.

SEXUAL (MIS)BEHAVIOR

In many of the larger species of shark,
the females have bite marks that may
be the result of males biting to
maintain their position while mating.
Some bite marks may also result from
courtship behavior in which the
males bite females to indicate their
interest in mating. The females of
some species have developed thicker
skin to protect themselves. No
comment necessary.

Asexual Reproduction

Parthenogenesis, or asexual reproduction,
has been noted in some female sharks
when males are not available. Pups
developed in this manner have no male
genetic contribution. The details of this
unusual process are unknown, but they
are thought to be a last-ditch effort to
reproduce when males are not around.

A female tiger shark with
mating bites on her flank.

What's it like
mating with a shark?
Let's just say it helps to
have a thick skin.

Arctic char

FISHY QUOTES

✦ *"A trout is a moment of beauty known only to those who seek it."* Arnold Gingrich

✦ *"Listen to the sound of the river and you will get a trout."* Irish proverb

✦ *"I fish because I love to; because I love the environs where trout are found, which are invariably beautiful…and, finally not because I regard fishing as being so terribly important, but because I suspect that so many of the other concerns of men are equally important—and not nearly so fun."* Robert Traver

✦ *"All the romance of trout fishing exists in the mind of the angler and is in no way shared by the fish."* Harold F. Blaisdell

Beautiful Char

These may be members of the char family, but that does not matter to trout anglers.

✦ **Lake trout:** These bruisers require cold water of 45 to 55°F (7 to 13°C). Unlike many other trout, they spawn in water deeper than 100 feet (30 meters). The female sweeps a depression in the bottom gravel and scatters her eggs. After 50 to 150 days, the few eggs not eaten by other fish hatch. The lucky few mature quickly and may live up to 40 years. This long life span accounts for their large average size of 20 pounds (9 kg), with the largest running to 100 pounds (45 kg).

✦ **Dolly Varden trout:** Take your pick of the origin of this trout's name. One theory is that it is named after the character of Dolly Varden in Charles Dickens's novel *Barnaby Rudge* (1840). Another possibility is that it comes from a type of dress that was popular in the 1870s. The Dolly Varden dress comprised a sheer overdress over a bright underdress. The effect was a shimmering glow, much like that of this trout's coloration.

✦ **Arctic char:** This northern fish can change its coloration depending on its environment. In rivers it has a dark coloration, while in the ocean it is lighter. This is a slow grower. It leaves rivers in summer and swims to the ocean for a few weeks of heavy feeding. During spawning, it develops a deep, bright red underside. In addition to its beauty, its red flesh is among the best in fishdom.

✦ **Brook trout:** A native of northeastern America, the beautiful brook trout has also been stocked in the cool waters of South America and Europe. It is valued for its sweet flesh on the table. Mature adults may be only 6 inches (15 cm) long, but a precious few four-year-olds may reach 5 pounds (2.3 kg) in weight.

Nothing in fishdom compares to the colors of a mature brook trout. Its back is dark green with pale olive worm-like markings. Its fins are orange with leading edges of white ahead of black stripes. Spread over its sides are tiny red dots surrounded by pale blue haloes.

Czech nymph

When Two (or Three) Are Better Than One

✤ **Droppers:** Fly fishermen often use two or three flies at the same time to offer a choice to the fish. The fly farthest from the angler is called the point fly. The others are called droppers; the one nearest the angler is the top dropper.

✤ **Dibbling:** When an angler uses three flies on a line, the one on top (the top dropper) can be danced (dibbled) on the surface in imitation of an insect trying to escape from the water.

CZECH THIS OUT

A recent addition to fly-fishing techniques comes from the Czechoslovakian international fly-fishing team. Czech nymphing involves presenting weighted flies down near the river bottom where trout rest. The weighted fly, known as a Czech nymph, was designed to attract the attention of resting trout, even when they were not actively feeding. As proof of its effectiveness, this method has been widely adopted by competitive and noncompetitive anglers alike. And you thought the only invention we have to thank the Czechs for was the sugar cube (1843).

SLOT LIMIT: NOTHING TO DO WITH LAS VEGAS

In order to protect some species, anglers must return fish that are under and over specified lengths to the water. Only those falling within the minimum and maximum allowable lengths may be kept. For example, the slot limit for sturgeon in Oregon is 38 to 54 inches (97 to 137 cm). Those not within this size range must be returned unharmed.

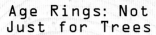

Age Rings: Not Just for Trees

Fish have ear stones— otoliths (calcium carbonate granules)— near their brains. Slicing through an ear stone allows for counting the formation rings. Each ring equals one year, so a fish's age can be determined by counting the rings. All vertebrates have them—even you and me— but they are unusually large in fish.

Cod

HOW CAPE COD GOT ITS NAME

To start with, a cape is any piece of land jutting into the sea. Cape Cod qualifies because it is one of the largest barrier islands in the world. In 1602, Englishman Bartholomew Gosnold noted the abundant "codfyshes" in the area. Today, the cod is the state fish of Massachusetts. A carved cod fish sits above the Massachusetts House of Representatives. The direction in which the cod faces, east or west, is determined by which political party is in the majority. Talk about something fishy in Massachusetts politics!

Cape Cod Bay

Cape Cod

A largemouth bass caught with a plastic worm on a drop-shot rig. Plastic worms have won more bass-fishing competitions than any other lure.

What's a Rig?

A rig is the arrangement of tackle, such as hooks, lures, weights, and swivels, at the end of the fishing line.

POPULAR WORM RIGS

❖ **Drop-shot rig:** The Japanese-designed drop-shot rig technique has the mainline tied to a sinker. A lure is tied to a leader above the sinker. This rigging technique allows the lure to sit at the exact depth of suspended fish.

❖ **Carolina rig:** The Carolina rig is a method for fishing a soft plastic lure along the bottom of a lake. It starts with a mainline and heavy sinker, then a bead and swivel. Next comes a leader with the plastic lure.

❖ **Florida rig:** A Florida rig has a sinker with a built-in metal corkscrew. It is screwed into a soft plastic worm, keeping the weight and lure tightly together and reducing tangles.

❖ **Mojo rig:** A mojo rig is designed for use with a spinning rod. It has cylindrical sinkers that can be retrieved through tumbles of rock without fouling.

❖ **Wacky rig:** Start with a straight-bodied soft plastic worm. Hook it through the middle, with the hook point exposed. This may look strange but it is effective for spawning fish. No one knows why.

Wacky rig

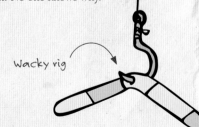

PHOTOGRAPHY: PROOF POSITIVE

Anglers with doubting friends can prove their expertise by photographing their catch. Only a few considerations need to be kept in mind to ensure a successful outcome for both the angler and the fish.

1) Keep the fish in the water until the photographer is ready to snap the picture.

2) The sun should be on the angler's face and behind the photographer.

3) Grasp the fish lightly at the head and tail, with the palms of the hands facing the photographer.

4) Do not place any fingers in the fish's gills, or grip the fish around its belly.

5) Lift the fish out of the water when the photographer is ready.

6) Shoot several pictures, filling the viewfinder of the camera with the angler and the fish, not the background.

7) Extend the fish toward the camera so that it will appear even larger than it is.

8) Return the fish carefully to the water.

9) Have 25 large glossy color prints made so that everyone you know can have a copy.

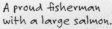
A proud fisherman with a large salmon.

Big Record— Small Boy: Big Fish

Seven-year-old Dylan Davis of Rowlett, Texas, caught a record 35-pound 10-ounce (16.2-kg) smallmouth buffalo. Rumor has it that his father held onto Dylan to prevent him from becoming the fish's lunch.

FISHY QUOTES

✦ "Fishermen are born honest, but they get over it." Ed Zern

✦ "We ask a simple question and that is all we wish: Are fishermen all liars? Or do only liars fish?" William Sherwood Fox

✦ "Of all the liars among mankind, the fisherman is the most trustworthy." William Sherwood Fox

✦ "All fishermen are liars; it's an occupational disease with them like housemaid's knee or editor's ulcers." Beatrice Cook

✦ "There is, among hard-core fishermen, a conviction that the truth, like pure water and the fish that live in it, is a precious commodity, not to be squandered or overused." Ed Zern

OVERCOMING THE OVERRUN

The backlash or overrun is the bane of every angler using a casting reel. The problem results when the reel's spool begins turning at too fast a rate to accommodate the outgoing line. As a result, the spool throws too much slack into the spooled line and, having nowhere to go, it tangles hopelessly. Some devotees suggest carrying a small darning needle to assist with removing the knots. The overrun was the single biggest explanation for the popularity of the overrunless spinning reel.

HOW FISH TASTE AND SMELL

Fish have chemoreceptors. They sense chemical stimulators in the water through the use of nares (receptors). Generally, these receptors are located on the lips, tongue, and mouth. Catfish, however, have receptors on their whiskers (barbels). The sensitivity of olfactory chemoreceptors varies by species—salmon, for example, can detect chemical levels as low as one part per billion. You were expecting the old joke, "How do you keep a fish from smelling? Cut off his nose," weren't you?

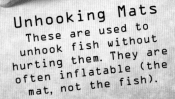

Unhooking Mats
These are used to unhook fish without hurting them. They are often inflatable (the mat, not the fish).

Male or Female? Yes

For reasons unknown, some fish species are hermaphrodites and change gender upon maturation. Cross-dressing is unknown.

Barramundi

✦ Barramundi: The barramundi, from estuaries, lagoons, and rivers in Australia, typically grows to 35 pounds (15.9 kg) and can attain a length of 6 feet (1.8 meters). It is favored as a table fish and larger specimens are becoming reduced due to overfishing. Barramundi are also used to stock freshwater lakes for recreational fishing. They start out as males but, after three to four years, most switch to females.

✦ Snook: This aggressive fish has mean looks to match its temperament. Heavyweights are up to 50 inches (127 cm) and 50 pounds (23 kg). The distinguishing characteristic is a dark line running the length of the silver body. Snook are commercially important due to their firm white meat. They are abundant and sexually mature at two years of age. Most males between two and seven years old change their gender. As a result, most of the very largest snook are females.

Aboriginal Fish

Aboriginal rock art depicting a barramundi at Kakadu National Park in northern Australia. The name barramundi comes from an Aboriginal word meaning large-scaled river fish.

Snook

Get Down to Get Bass

+ Bass seldom suspend in the water column; they prefer the bottom or something that signifies the bottom. This could be a weed bed, dock pilings, rocks, tires, wood, bushes, sunken objects, or anything "different" from the bottom. Bass that are ready to feed will be closest to the bottom or structure. Finding structure is the key to finding feeding bass. Virtually every serious bass angler will have electronics onboard to show the available structure.

+ Bass spend much of the year near shallow spawning areas. These areas are flat, with some cover, and with fast access to deep water. Bass beds are easily seen by anglers. Bigger bass generally make their nests in relatively deeper water.

+ Bass are schooling fish, and bass of the same size school together. The deeper the depth, the tighter the school. If you catch one, you can be sure that there are others in the immediate area, so fish carefully at the same depth. One frightened bass can scare off the entire school. If you catch a bass but do not wish to keep it, put it in a live well rather than releasing it immediately. As soon as you release it, it will rejoin the school and frighten them into the next county.

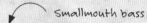

Smallmouth bass

Tim Knepp

Largemouth bass caught on a fly rod and popping bug (a floating fly made for bass angling).

PREFERRED BASS COVER

• Wood, including standing timber, fallen trees, stumps, brush, logs, logjams, and man-made wood structure such as docks and pilings
• Weeds, including hydrilla, lily pads, floating weeds such as hyacinths, grasses, subsurface grasses (milfoil, hydrilla, and coontail), and mosses
• Rocks

WHERE TO FIND BASS

✦ **Rivers:** The higher level of dissolved oxygen in rivers provides good conditions for bass. Being slightly warmer in winter and slightly cooler in summer, rivers have more favorable temperatures year-round than do lakes. Bass will be found out of the major currents but closer to shorelines. Large objects, such as boulders in midstream, provide shelter for bass and act as a conveyor belt bringing food to the hiding bass.

✦ **Streams:** Smallmouth bass rather than largemouth can be found in cooler streams. They will take up residence in the holes below rapids and along steep rock walls. Undercut banks also provide slower water and shelter.

✦ **Reservoirs:** The cyclical changing water levels due to drawdowns (water usage) mean that weed beds are unable to be established, so the bass orient to other structure such as flooded timber. Other prime areas include old river channels, submerged islands, and old roadbeds. Reservoirs stratify in warm weather and this presents a problem—too little oxygen. Bass will avoid this zone, so the angler who knows this depth will avoid it and fish the more preferred depth.

✦ **Ponds:** Ponds are not often subject to changes in water levels. For this reason, the shoreline is an important area for bass. Vegetation and fallen trees provide ambush cover near shorelines. Some ponds are subject to heavy vegetation, making fishing difficult, but at the same time, heavy vegetation makes better bass habitat.

Fly Lines

Fly lines are available in a range of weights, configurations, and functions. Knowing which to select improves the angler's success, because the appropriate line can better deliver the fly. The first distinction is the floating versus sinking lines. The next major distinction is the profile. Some are tapered at both ends and made for gentler presentations of the fly as well as allowing the angler to use the "reserve" end when the first wears out. Others have varying degrees of weight concentrated at the front end to aid in distance casting.

Lines come in many colors to match the angler's mood.

Backing

The typical fly line is 90 feet (27 meters) long. When fishing for larger fish, it may be possible for the fish to take out all of the line. To prevent it from being broken off when the fish hits the end of the line, fly fishermen wind 300 feet (91 meters) of a thin line known as backing onto the reel before the fly line is added. This way the angler has an abundance of line should the fish run out.

Some Types of Fly Lines

❖ **Level:** Constant diameter from end to end.

❖ **Double taper:** Thin, tapered ends and a fatter center section.

❖ **Weight forward:** Much of the line's weight is built into the front half of the line.

❖ **Triangle taper:** Has an elongated weight-forward section.

❖ **Shooting taper:** Extremely heavy forward section connected to a very thin rear section.

❖ **Long belly:** Has a very elongated weight-forward taper.

❖ **Bass taper:** Heavier weight line with much of the weight concentrated up front.

❖ **Sink tip:** Forward section sinks while remainder floats.

❖ **Sinking:** These sink at different rates, including intermediate, fast sinking, and depth charge.

❖ **Saltwater:** For heavyweight rods required for larger fish.

STRIPED BASS: UNINTENDED TRAVELER

✤ **Popular names:** Striped bass are also known as stripers, rocks, rockfish, striped sea bass, linesiders, squid hounds, and greenheads.

✤ **Distribution:** Striped bass are a true bass, once native only to the Atlantic coast. In 1879, the United States Fish Commission stocked striped bass fry on the Pacific coast. Damming of rivers trapped many spawning fish in lakes above the dams. Since that time they have been planted in many freshwater lakes.

✤ **Spawning:** Striped bass leave the ocean and spawn in freshwater rivers when the water reaches 60°F (15°C). Stripers do not build nests. Instead, several males surround a female and eggs are fertilized as they drift free of the female. Depending on her size, a female will produce 60,000 to 5 million eggs, but only a fraction of them will survive to adulthood.

Myths About Freshwater Stripers

♦ *Stripers eat black bass and crappie.* Rarely—they prefer shad.

♦ *Stripers eat their own weight in baitfish each day.* Nothing in nature eats its own weight in a day. Stripers eat 3 to 5 percent of their weight per day. A 20-pound (9-kg) striper eats about 1 pound (0.45 kg) per day.

♦ *Stripers eat 24/7.* Stripers go on feeding cycles like any other fish.

♦ *Stripers are not good to eat.* Stripers make excellent table fish—if you enjoy fish for dinner.

Catching a Striper

★ Stripers of 50 pounds (23 kg) are commonly caught in freshwater lakes. The IGFA world record is 81 pounds 14 ounces (37.14 kg), taken in Long Island Sound between New York and Connecticut.

★ The lubricant WD-40 is used by striped bass anglers targeting stripers during their post-spawning feeding binge in the Hudson River. The attractant is sprayed onto lures and even on livebait such as sand worms. Why does it work? Maybe it is just something different and the fish are curious.

Freshly caught striped bass.

An angler releasing an Atlantic salmon back to the river to spawn.

ATLANTIC SALMON: SPORT FISH OF KINGS

* The Atlantic salmon's scientific name is *Salmo salar*. Some claim it means "the leaper" because of the fish's determination when ascending falls as it migrates upstream during its spawning run. Others, with less imagination, claim that its name means "from salt water."

* The Atlantic's original range was from Greenland to Connecticut and from Russia to Portugal. Overharvesting and pollution has reduced these once prolific runs to a remnant of their original size. In the United States, Atlantic salmon fishing is limited to only New York (Lake Ontario) and Michigan (Lake Michigan), where the Atlantics have been reintroduced. Canada enjoys salmon fishing in its maritime provinces. Britain and Europe continue to offer sport fishing for Atlantics.

* Atlantic salmon tradition holds that it is done by fly fishing. Salmon will take either wet (sinking) or dry (floating) flies. The strategy is to restrict your fishing to areas where salmon are known to congregate; this is why a guide will be invaluable. River guides know where the fish will be. Year after year, the same holding areas will contain fish, while other areas will be devoid of them.

Pacific Salmon and Their Sizes

♦ **Chum**, also known as dog salmon because they are fed to sled dogs—10 to 20 pounds (4.5 to 9 kg)

♦ **Sockeye**, also known as reds for their body color during spawning—4 to 8 pounds (1.8 to 3.6 kg)

♦ **Kokanee**, the midget landlocked version of the sockeye—less than 4 pounds (1.8 kg)

♦ **Pink** or **humpback**—4 to 6 pounds (1.8 to 2.7 kg)

♦ **Coho**, also known as silvers for their color—up to 30 pounds (13.6 kg)

♦ **Chinook**, also known as king due to their large size—15 to 35 pounds (6.8 to 15.9 kg), with a commercial-catch record of 125 pounds (57 kg)

Spawning chinook salmon

Atlantic salmon →

BOOM TO BUST

Runs of migrating Atlantic salmon during colonial times were so great that American colonists netted, speared, and pitchforked them by the wagon load. Some were eaten fresh, but most were dried and preserved for later consumption. So easy was it to collect this bounty that indentured servants had written into their contracts that they would be served salmon no more than four times per week.

FISHING WEIR

A fishing weir is an obstruction, traditionally constructed from wooden stakes or stones, that is placed in rivers, estuaries, or tidal waters. It can be used to redirect or trap fish. A fishing weir is often used to capture adult migrating fish on their upstream spawning run. Hardly seems fair, does it?

← Salmon weir on the Cowichan River, Vancouver Island, c. 1866.

Differences Between Salmon and Trout Fishing

Trout anglers who use trout tactics to fish for salmon will often come up empty.

+ Trout anglers have to strike quickly to hook a trout. After years of such habit, it is often difficult for trout anglers to hook salmon. Striking a salmon too quickly will pull the fly from its mouth.

+ Trout anglers present their flies to feeding fish. Knowledge of what insects are hatching often makes trout angling fast and furious, with many fish landed and released in a day. Salmon, however, are not feeding when they return to the river to migrate and spawn. It is common to cast many times to salmon before they become angry enough to take the fly.

+ Trout prefer to lay in areas where the current can carry food to them. Salmon prefer to avoid such places, and rest in calm areas where they can stay away from the river's current. This is why a salmon guide is important in finding salmon holding areas.

Fish Named for Other Things

Given the abundance of fish, it makes sense that naming fish should rely on a similarity to other things in the environment. However, given the unusual names for some fish, one has to wonder what the namers were thinking.

- ✛ Angelfish
- ✛ Bonefish
- ✛ Butterfish
- ✛ Candlefish
- ✛ Chain pickerel
- ✛ Clownfish
- ✛ Cornetfish
- ✛ Drum
- ✛ Filefish
- ✛ Gnomefish
- ✛ Guitarfish
- ✛ Hammerhead shark

- ✛ Knifefish
- ✛ Leaffish
- ✛ Milk shark
- ✛ Milkfish
- ✛ Needlefish
- ✛ Pike
- ✛ Puddingwife
- ✛ Pumpkinseed
- ✛ Ribbonfish
- ✛ Rockfish
- ✛ Rubyfish
- ✛ Sailfin molly

- ✛ Sailfish
- ✛ Sawfish
- ✛ Sawtail catshark
- ✛ Scabbardfish
- ✛ Skate
- ✛ Spadefish
- ✛ Spearfish
- ✛ Star-studded grouper
- ✛ Stargazer
- ✛ Sunfish
- ✛ Surfperch
- ✛ Swordfish

- ✛ Threadfin
- ✛ Tilefish
- ✛ Triggerfish
- ✛ Trunkfish
- ✛ Tuskfish
- ✛ Wedgefish
- ✛ Wreckfish

The triggerfish can raise two of its sharp dorsal spines as protection from predators. The first spine can only be lowered by pressing the second spine, which acts as a trigger.

The sawfish is a shark-like ray and is named for its long, toothy snout that looks like a saw.

"Man Fishing a New England Stream" by Winslow Homer, watercolor, c. 1880–1910.

A River Runs Through It

❖ This 1976 book is a semi-autobiographical account by Norman Maclean, telling of his family in the early 1900s.

❖ The often quoted opening passage reads, "In our family, there was no clear line between religion and fly fishing. We lived at the junction of great trout rivers in western Montana, and our father was a Presbyterian minister and a fly fisherman who tied his own flies and taught others. He told us about Christ's disciples being fishermen, and we were left to assume, as my brother and I did, that all first-class fishermen on the Sea of Galilee were fly fishermen and that John, the favorite, was a dry fly fisherman."

❖ The 1992 film of the same name singlehandedly sent the cost of fly-fishing equipment through the roof. Directed by Robert Redford, it won an Academy Award for best cinematography and was nominated for two others. As a result of its success, the demand for fly tackle was at an all-time high. Of course, the demand has since gone down but the prices have not.

Angling in Art

WINSLOW HOMER, CONSIDERED ONE OF THE MOST IMPORTANT PAINTERS OF THE 1800s, WAS KNOWN FOR HIS OUTDOOR PAINTINGS. HE WAS ALSO A FLY FISHERMAN.

SONGS WITH FISH IN THE TITLE

- Anchovy In The UK
- Cod Only Knows
- Cod You Be Love
- Crappie Birthday
- Don't Go Baking My Carp
- Fish You Were Here
- Guppy Love
- Hake Rattle And Roll
- I Lobster And Never Flounder
- I'm A Sole Man
- Islands In The Bream
- Lings Can Only Get Battered
- Never Mind The Pollocks
- Papa Don't Perch
- Ray Of Light
- Salmon Chanted Evening
- Salmon When We Touch
- Send In The Clownfish
- Shark The Herald
  Angels Ling
- Sitting On The Haddock
  Of The Bay
- Small Town Koi
- Sprat! In The Name Of Love
- That's A Moray
- The Herring Cycle
- The Kray You Make Me Eel
- The Ray We Were
- Walk This Ray
- Walleye Wait For You
- We've Gotta Get Out
  Of This Plaice
- Whale Meet Again
- When A Man Loves A Gudgeon
- You Can Tune A Piano
  But You Can't Tuna Fish

Mud Feet

These are disks placed under the legs of a seat box in order to prevent the legs from sinking into soft mud and upending the angler.

Art Flick's Streamside Guide

First published in 1947, angler Art Flick's *Streamside Guide* became an instant classic because it showed photographs of every important aquatic insect from his home waters, the Catskill rivers in New York. He also included photographs of each life stage for each insect, along with photographs and instructions for tying each imitation. His book has been republished many times and is still available today. Flick invented many fly patterns, and for this he is regarded as an American fly-fishing luminary.

Mayflies by a stream.

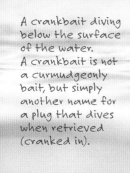
A crankbait diving below the surface of the water. A crankbait is not a curmudgeonly bait, but simply another name for a plug that dives when retrieved (cranked in).

PLUG TECHNIQUES

Plugs are designed either to float on the surface, dive when retrieved, or sink. Different plugs can also be retrieved in many ways—slow, fast, or any speed in between. These factors make them very versatile lures for predatory fish.

✦ **Topwater (or surface) plugs:** These float on top of the water both when retrieved and at rest. Fishing topwater plugs is exciting because the explosive strike is visible. Predatory fish such as bass often stun their prey, so the entire process happens before your eyes. Experimenting with different speeds of retrieve is the way to decide which method the fish prefer on that particular day. Often, the slightest twitch, not really a retrieve, will bring the fish to the surface.

✦ **Divers (lipped plugs):** These plugs dive under the surface when retrieved and float to the top when at rest. A plug with a large lip will dive deeply and quickly, while a plug with a smaller lip will remain nearer the surface.

✦ **Sinking plugs:** These are weighted plugs that sink when at rest and maintain their depth when retrieved.

Warm-water Spawning Lineup: Who's On First?

Not all species of warm-water fish spawn at the same time. Knowing the order of spawning may help you to target species that are especially active either before or after the spawn. Here is the order for spawning warm-water fish:

1) Northern pike

2) Walleye

3) Yellow perch

4) Smallmouth/black crappie/ white crappie

5) Largemouth bass

6) Sunfish/bluegill/pumpkinseed

7) Catfish

The northern pike is the first warm-water fish to spawn.

CHANNEL CATFISH

The channel catfish is the most abundant sport fish in the midwestern United States. The state of Iowa, for example, boasts populations from 500 to 5,000 pounds (225 to 2,250 kg) of catfish per mile of streams. The largest fish are found in lakes and ponds. Channel catfish are so popular as dinner fare that they are also known as prairie trout. There was once a campaign to advertise them as prairie escargots, but it never caught on.

Channel catfish— a very tasty late spawner.

Mounted Fish: No Saddle Necessary

If photographs are not enough, an angler can get a 3D reminder of a trophy fish.

A stuffed and mounted king salmon.

TRADITIONAL TAXIDERMY PROCESS

A skilled taxidermist will:

1) Take photographs for reference, and measure length and girth.

2) Remove the skin in one piece, making the incision on the side that will be against the wall and hidden from view.

3) Cure the skin to prevent deterioration. All color is lost during this process.

4) Pack the skin with an inert filling or place it on a commercial form.

5) Stitch the skin together along the original incision.

6) Paint the skin to restore the fish's original colors.

ALTERNATIVE PROCESS

Immediately after catching the fish, the angler should:

1) Take many photographs, including close-up details, and measure the fish.

2) Return the fish, unharmed, to the water.

3) Send the photographs and measurements to a taxidermist, who will provide a fiberglass replica of the fish, true to size and coloration.

4) The angler is happy with this trophy; the fish is happy for its freedom; the taxidermist is happy for the work—and all is right with the world.

In taxidermy, the last step of painting the fish is critical. A skilled taxidermist can make the mount come alive instead of look like a rubber fish.

Strange Sturgeon Secrets

❖ Sturgeon have been with us since the age of the dinosaurs. They appeared in the fossil record 200 million years ago and are virtually unchanged since that time.

❖ Sturgeon can live to be 100 years old.

❖ Sturgeon of the Caspian Sea reportedly attain 20 feet (6 meters) in length and weigh up to 4,400 pounds (1,996 kg), making them among the largest fish in the world.

❖ The record rod and reel sturgeon was caught in the Fraser River in British Columbia. It reportedly measured 20 feet (6 meters) long and weighed 1,832 pounds (831 kg).

❖ In spite of their size, sturgeon have no teeth and need none because they suck up insects, small invertebrates, and the occasional crayfish off the bottom.

❖ The sturgeon has no scales. It is covered with five rows of large bony plates, making the fish pentagon-shaped (five-sided) in cross-section.

❖ For the most part sturgeon are anadromous—that is, they live in both fresh and salt water.

❖ Sturgeon are native to subtropical, temperate, and subarctic rivers, lakes, and coastlines of North America and Eurasia. They are everywhere, I tell you, everywhere.

❖ Sturgeon is very desirable as a table fish and many subspecies are valued for their eggs (caviar).

❖ Sturgeon lay as much as 200 pounds (91 kg) of eggs per female.

❖ Pound for pound, sturgeon eggs made into caviar makes sturgeon the most expensive of all harvested fish.

❖ Due to their desirability, slow growth rate, and overfishing, sturgeon is the most endangered fish in the world. In many places, if one is caught it must be returned because it is a protected species.

❖ In Washington and Oregon, the legal size for sturgeon is between 38 and 54 inches (97 and 137 cm). Fish larger or smaller than this range must be returned unharmed.

Caviar

Sometimes called black caviar, this is one of the most expensive luxuries among all piscatorial pleasures. These are the eggs of wild sturgeon from the Caspian and Black seas. The highest quality roe (eggs) is salted, non-fertilized, and non-pasteurized. The cost of prime caviar can be $8,000 to $16,000 per kilogram (2.2 pounds).

TYPES OF STURGEON

This ancient fish is widely distributed and there are more than 20 separate types:

- Adriatic
- Alabama
- Amur
- Atlantic
- Baikal
- Beluga
- Chinese
- Dwarf
- European
- Fringebarbel
- Green
- Gulf
- Japanese
- Kaluga
- Lake
- Pallid
- Persian
- Russian
- Sakhalin
- Shortnose
- Shovelnose
- Siberian
- Starry
- Sterlet
- White
- Yangtze

Sturgeons are covered in rows of armored body plates and have barbels (whiskers) for bottom feeding.

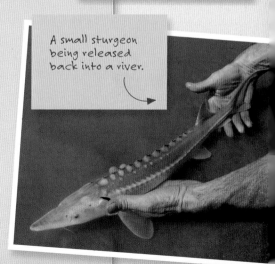

A small sturgeon being released back into a river.

Permit

Permit are adaptable and can be found over soft or rocky bottoms, offshore in deep water, or on shallow flats. They root on the bottom and eat mollusks, urchins, crabs, and shrimp. They have no teeth. Instead, the roof of their mouth is a hard plate for crushing their prey. So strong are permit that they can crush an angler's hook flat. Permit is sought after as a table fish. When on the flats (in shallow, sandy-bottomed water), it is targeted by anglers and has the reputation of being a very wary fish, easily spooked. With its wide, deep body, it is a difficult fish to catch. The IGFA world record is 60 pounds (27.21 kg).

Pompano: Miniature Permit

Pompano belong to the same family as permit—they are both part of the *Trachinotus* genus of the Carangidae family (also known as jacks). The pompano's compact oval body gives it a fighting ability that anglers desire. It inhabits very shallow water and is accessible to anglers fishing from the beach or from bridges. Florida pompano average 2 pounds (0.9 kg) and can be found—where else?—along the entire west coast of Florida.

A school of pompano.

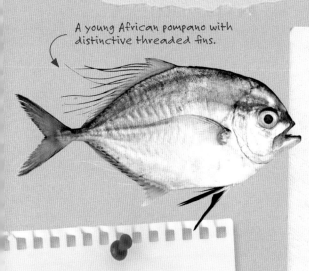

A young African pompano with distinctive threaded fins.

AFRICAN POMPANO

African pompano are part of the *Alectis* genus of the Carangidae (jacks) family. This fish is silvery metallic-blue to blue-green above and silver below. Its body is deep and thin. Also known as threadfin trevally, the juveniles of this species display long threads on their dorsal and anal fins. The young live at sea and will grow to 3 feet (90 cm) and 40 pounds (18.1 kg). They are prized for their fight and are good to eat.

TENKARA FISHING

Tenkara, a simplified version of fly fishing, was originally promoted to encourage Japanese samurai warriors to use their time peacefully when not engaged in wars. This style of small-stream fly fishing is enjoying a resurgence today, due to its simplified style. It uses no reel. Instead, the line is attached directly to the rod tip. If this were sufficient to calm the warriors, imagine what it could do for normal folk.

The World's Fishing Fleet

As of 2002, there were 4 million vessels in the world's fishing fleet, 80 percent of which was Asian. Only 1 percent is larger than 80 feet (24 meters), and half of these larger vessels are in China.

GROUNDBAITS

Groundbaits, originally developed by match anglers, are used to attract and keep fish in the area so that they can be caught by the angler—a process referred to as prebaiting. The groundbait ingredients are moistened and formed into balls that are then cast into the water. The balls either sink to the bottom before breaking up, or they break up into a cloud of particles while sinking (known as cloudbait).

Groundbait mixture

FISHY QUOTES

+ *"I don't want to sit at the head table anymore. I want to go fishing."* George Bush

+ *"There is always something wonderful about a new fishing adventure trip. Fishing is like Jason's quest for the Golden Fleece."* Zane Grey

+ *"No fisherman ever fishes as much as he wants to."* Geoffrey Norman

+ *"No life is so happy and so pleasant as the life of the well-gover'd angler."* Izaak Walton

+ *"Many of the most highly publicized events of my presidency are not nearly as memorable or significant in my life as fishing with my daddy."* Jimmy Carter

+ *"The only reason I ever played golf in the first place was so that I could go fishing."* Sam Snead

SOME GROUNDBAIT INGREDIENTS

Groundbaits contain interesting ingredients, such as breadcrumbs, maggots, pigeon droppings, crushed hemp, ground peanuts, ground maize, and crushed biscuits—all four of the basic food groups.

* **Grilled hemp seeds:** This is a favored groundbait additive. Its oily texture attracts tench, chub, carp, and roach. Prior to adding hemp to groundbait, it can be grilled and crushed, which is believed to be more effective than ungrilled hemp. Breathing in the smoke is not considered a violation.

* **Damp leam:** When mixed with groundbait, this fine-particled clay takes the bait straight to the bottom and slowly releases the bait. A favorite of match anglers, it attracts fish and keeps them close by the angler. Not to be confused with wet or dry leam.

* **Peat:** Peat is an additive for making a groundbait that gives off a dark cloud without adding any food value.

BALLING IN

+ This is the process of throwing or catapulting groundbait or loosebait, such as boilies, maggots, or casters, into a desired area prior to fishing.

+ A loosefeed catapult (slingshot) is often used to broadcast the bait farther than could be thrown by hand alone.

+ A polecat is a one-handed catapult for delivering the bait while holding a long pole.

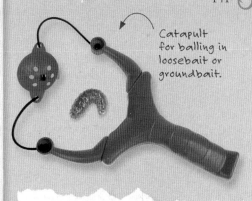

Catapult for balling in loosebait or groundbait.

Polecat—a type of catapult as well as a colloquialism for a skunk.

Swimfeeders and Bait Droppers

Swimfeeders and bait droppers are used to slowly release groundbait under the rod or pole tip when fishing. They are widely used when ledgering for fish. A swimfeeder is simply a plastic or metal cage, while a bait dropper is a small plastic or metal apparatus that is designed to release the bait when it reaches the bottom.

RHYTHM METHOD (NOT THE ONE APPROVED BY THE POPE)

When summer fishing at mid-depth, broadcasting maggots over the surface and striking repeatedly until a fish is hooked is known as the rhythm method. The broadcasting keeps the fish actively feeding as the bait sinks to the depth where the baited hook is holding.

Swimfeeder

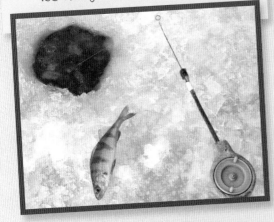
Ice fishing for yellow perch.

The Palatable Perch

+ **Behavior:** Perch do not make nests for spawning. Instead, they lay their eggs in a string over weeds. From then on, the eggs and hatchlings are on their own. As a result, only one fry out of 5,000 will make it to one year old. Year-class fish, or similarly sized fish, will travel together in schools.

+ **Through the ice:** Ice fishing for perch is a favorite winter pastime for anglers. Tip-ups (ice traps) baited with 3-inch (7.5-cm) minnows or small jigs and spoons in shallow water work well. Ice anglers know that perch is a very light-striking fish, so they set the hook (secure the hook in the fish's mouth) at the slightest touch on the bait. With a little luck, a few hours on the ice can yield a year's worth of sweet meat for the freezer.

YELLOW PERCH

Yellow perch from cold water are a delight on the table, so it is a good thing that there are lots of them around because they only grow 2 or 3 inches (5 or 7.5 cm) per year. They average 9 inches (23 cm) and weigh less than a pound (0.45 kg). However, some rocky lakes with sandy bottoms may produce perch weighing over 2 pounds (0.9 kg).

Yellow perch

Well Fish

During the Middle Ages, trout were kept in wells to eat insects and keep the water potable. The well trout was an earlier version of the canary in the mine, warning of pollution by their demise.

Fish Oil and Health

Fish oil is separated from fish solids in a kind of rendering plant. The solids go off to become fish fertilizer. The oil is more valuable than petroleum and sells for more than twice the price of crude oil. The liquid, called stickwater, is skimmed off after being centrifuged. Many people take fish oil supplements because the omega-3 fatty acids are believed to be effective treatments for arthritis by reducing inflammation and pain. Studies of these benefits are inconclusive.

Mass-produced Fishing Rods

Mass production keeps the cost of fishing rods down and provides consistency in quality. Long fibers of fiberglass, boron, or titanium are applied to a flat sheet of fiberglass. The thickness and number of fibers determine the strength and flexibility of the finished product. The sheet of material is then wrapped around a tapered steel rod called a mandrel. The diameter of the mandrel also influences the flexibility of the finished rod. The glass-covered mandrel is baked in an industrial oven. The heat bonds the fibers together. When the mandrel is removed, the hollow rod form is ready for trimming and application of hardware.

Selection of mass-produced saltwater fishing rods.

The Robust Brown Trout

+ Browns are originally from Europe and North Africa, and were introduced to North America in 1882. Thousands of eggs were imported to Massachusetts, but only three fish survived. These three fish became the source of today's thriving brown trout fishery in the United States.

+ Browns can adapt to less than ideal water conditions. They can tolerate water that is too warm for other trout species. With higher temperatures comes lower dissolved oxygen, which would kill other trout but not the brown. Poorer water quality that would spell the end for other trout is also tolerated by browns.

+ Unlike all other trout, brown trout are cannibalistic toward their own young—they just cannot pass up an easy lunch. Eager to strike a fly, brown trout have been favored by fly fishermen since the 15th century.

+ Big brown trout, the kind that make for a trophy fish, are much more active after dark. Knowledgeable anglers quietly listen for the sound of big browns chasing baitfish in the shallows. A large fly is then cast so as to cover the area where the big brown is working. Fly color is less important than the size of the fly. A large fly that will move a lot of water is preferred and a heavy tippet (the thin end of the leader line to which the fly is tied) is required for the chance at a once-in-a-lifetime fish. The IGFA world record is 41 pounds 8 ounces (18.82 kg).

A large brown trout caught while fly fishing in Argentina.

SEA TROUT
The sea trout is a silvery colored sea-going form of the brown trout.

FISHY QUOTES

✦ *"The best way to learn to be a fly fisherman is to go to a river and ask the trout for a few lessons."* Gwen Cooper

✦ *"I look into my flybox and think about all the elements I should consider in choosing the perfect fly: water temp, what stage of development the bugs are in, what the fish are eating right now. Then, I remember what a guide once told me—90% of what a trout eats is brown and fuzzy and about 3/8 inch long."* Allison Moir

✦ *"Trout are not looking for something new and different to eat or do."* Arnold Gingrich

✦ *"There's no taking of trout with dry breeches."* Miguel de Cervantes

✦ *"Most anglers spend their lives in making rules for trout, and trout spend theirs in breaking them."* George Aston

✦ *"On average, trout fishermen will walk about as far from the parking lot as sunbathers."* M.R. Montgomery

✦ *"A trout that doesn't think two jumps and several runs ahead of the average fisherman is mighty apt to get fried."* Beatrice Cook

✦ *"Many a beginner who cracks off his flies pleasures himself with the idea that some trout of large dimensions has carried them away."* W.C. Stewart

Fish in Chinese Art

★ The yin/yang symbol is a common one in Chinese art and often represents wealth. It shows a stylized figure of two fish, a red one with its head facing up to signify growth, and a black one facing down to balance that energy.

★ Another common Chinese symbol shows three fish, head to tail, representing eternity and a cyclical series of new beginnings.

Symbol of eternity

HOW DO GILLS WORK?

Gills and lungs have similar functions—
to take in oxygen and release carbon
dioxide. Both have thin blood vessels
with thin walls very close to the surface.
Gases such as oxygen and carbon
dioxide can pass through the walls. The
air we breathe has 200,000 parts per
million oxygen. Water has only four to
eight parts per million oxygen, so fish
have a more difficult time exchanging
the gases than we do. As a result, fish
have to keep on the move constantly to
get the oxygen they need. It also means
that fish cannot sleep as we do; they
need to have water constantly moving
across their gills to live.

The gills of a giant catfish.

Beaching
This is a technique for
landing fish by leading
them into shallow water,
where they can be
controlled and either
netted or released.

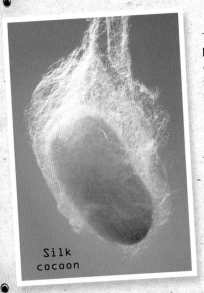

Silk
cocoon

PEARSALL'S SILK

The use of silk thread in fly tying goes back to
Dame Juliana Berners' 15th-century "Treatyse
of Fysshynge Wyth an Angle." Pearsall's pure
silk tying threads and flosses have been in
demand by fly-tying luminaries for the past
200 years, and many patterns insist on Pearsall's.
Silk does not change color, as do synthetics.
Furthermore, wet silk has a translucent and
iridescent characteristic that is unmatched by
synthetics. While some competitors use waste
silk, Pearsall's uses raw silk hundreds or even
thousands of yards long. These raw fibers are
obtained by unwinding the cocoon of the silk
worm. They're not happy about it but what
can they do—they're only worms.

ATLANTIC MACKEREL: SPEEDY STRIKERS

This open-ocean speedster travels in schools of thousands. Mackerel can live up to 20 years and reach nearly 8 pounds (3.6 kg). Females reach sexual maturity at age three, and each can produce up to a million eggs. They cruise the mid-depth of the continental shelves and seldom travel deeper than 600 feet (183 meters). Experienced anglers know that mackerel strike hard and then release their prey before swallowing it. The best technique is to wait for the second strike before setting the hook.

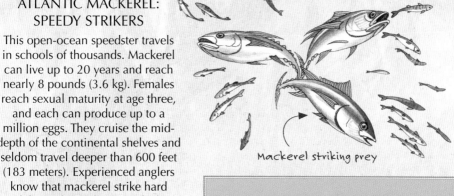

Mackerel striking prey

Setting the Hook a.k.a. Striking

Striking is a sweeping motion of the rod tip in order to tighten the line and set (secure) the hook in the fish's mouth. Striking is also the term used for a fish's attack on bait, lure, or fly. It is also the term for knocking all the pins down with one roll of the bowling ball, but that is neither here nor there.

Mackerel are a popular target species for anglers, but also make excellent bait-fish for larger fish.

Stickbait

STICKBAITS ARE PLUG LURES THAT IMITATE INJURED MINNOWS. MADE FROM HARD PLASTIC, THEY MAY FLOAT OR SINK, DEPENDING ON THEIR CONSTRUCTION. THEY ARE RETRIEVED WITH SHORT JERKS, IMITATING AN INJURED PREY FISH, AND TAKE ADVANTAGE OF A PREDATORY FISH'S WILLINGNESS TO MAKE AN EASY MEAL OF A WOUNDED FISH.

Spinner   Spinnerbait   Spoon

SPINNERS AND SPOONS

These lures are designed to provoke predatory fish to strike. The weight of the lure aids casting and helps the lure to sink. When retrieved, the lure spins or flutters in imitation of a baitfish.

★ **Spinners:** Consisting of a central wire axis covered by a metal cylindrical body, these have a blade that revolves around the center wire. Depth is controlled by the rate of retrieve.

★ **Spinnerbaits:** Also known as buzzbaits or wirebaits, these consist of metal wire arms shaped like an open safety pin. One leg of the pin has a hook surrounded by a rubber skirt. The other leg has one or more metal blades that flutter and create a commotion when retrieved. Different shapes of blade produce different kinds of disturbance. The noise of the spinnerbait attracts the fish's attention and goads it into striking. They are usually fished near the surface with a fast retrieve.

★ **Spoons:** These are made from a flat piece of metal, which is often formed into a gentle curve so that the lure flutters when retrieved.

Keepnet: Essence of Great Expectations

A KEEPNET IS A SUBMERGED NYLON HOLDING PEN INTO WHICH FISH ARE RELEASED AFTER THEY HAVE BEEN SCORED FOR PURPOSES OF DETERMINING THE MATCH WINNER IN AN ANGLING COMPETITION. TYPICALLY, THE SIZE OF THE KEEPNET IS PROPORTIONAL TO THE ANGLER'S OPINION OF HIM/HERSELF.

An angler using a landing net to lift his catch into a keepnet.

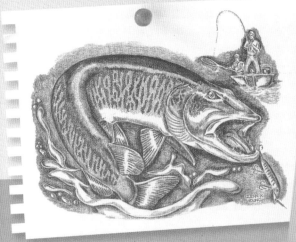

Muskie—the fish of a thousand casts.

Use needle-nose pliers to unhook a muskie safely.

MUSKELLUNGE

❖ Muskies are the biggest and fastest growing of the pike family. They can reach 70 pounds (32 kg) and may live to eight years. In lakes, this big fish requires five acres of feeding space to maintain its rapid growth rate. In rivers, muskies take up housekeeping in deep holes near where another stream comes in. This area receives any food being brought in by the incoming current.

❖ A 5-foot (1.5-meter), 60-pound (27-kg) muskie requires a heavy-duty rod and bait-casting reel loaded with 300 feet (91 meters) of 20-pound (9-kg) test line. Springtime anglers use a big spinner that moves a lot of water and makes plenty of noise. Come summer, muskie anglers use 8- to 12-inch (20- to 30-cm) suckers for bait. Equally big floating plugs, jerked rapidly across the surface, can entice a strike.

❖ Impatient anglers do not hook many muskies. A suspended muskie, even if it can be seen in the water, may require 20 or more casts before it will strike. Retrieves must be erratic to interest a muskie. Constant speed on the retrieve will not provoke a strike. Repeated casts to suspected holding areas will increase an angler's odds of success.

Inventor of the Outboard Motor

Although often mistakenly credited to Ole Evinrude, the outboard motor was invented by Cameron Waterman in 1903. It was capable of propelling a 12- to 16-foot (3.7- to 4.9-meter) boat at 6 to 8 miles per hour (9.7 to 12.9 kph). His invention was patented 1905.

Wild Carp

Also known as wildies, these are the rare descendants of carp bred by monks in the Middle Ages (I swear this is true). Their range is very limited and they are found in very few waters.

Wild carp

Sorry to carp so much, but I feel like a fish out of water sitting here.

Asian Carp: Flying to Waters Near You

Several varieties of Asian carp are invasive species in North America and are eliminating native species. These carp can grow to 4 feet (1.2 meters) and can weigh 100 pounds (45 kg). They are destroying ecosystems by starving out other varieties of fish. An ever-growing problem in particular is the jumping carp. The fish jump clear of the water when frightened, and have been known to collide with boaters and cause serious injuries to the operators.

FISHY EXPRESSIONS

Everyday expressions employing fishy phrases run the gamut from mundane to ridiculous.

- Something sounds fishy— *something suspicious*
- Like a fish out of water—*awkward*
- Fishing for a compliment— *in search of praise*
- Fish or cut bait—*encouragement to make up one's mind*
- Going on a fishing expedition— *an effort to discover facts*
- Red herring—*intentional misdirection*
- Holy mackerel!—*an exclamation of surprise*
- Like shooting fish in a barrel—*an exceptionally easy task*
- Green around the gills—*showing obvious discomfort*
- Living in a fishbowl—*to have one's life open for examination*
- Packed in like sardines— *extremely crowded*
- Cold fish—*one lacking in interpersonal warmth*
- Drinks like a fish—*to over-imbibe*
- Fine kettle of fish—*an annoying problem*
- Big fish in a small pond—*one who is important within a limited circle of influence*
- Plenty of other fish in the sea— *other possibilities abound*
- Carp about something—*find fault or make niggling complaints*

Fishing in India

Angling in India includes two interesting species.

Rohu

- **Golden mahseer:** This fish is excellent on the table and has been known to attain 9 feet (2.7 meters) and 119 pounds (54 kg). It is noted for its fighting ability when hooked.

- **Rohu:** Unlike many other fish, this member of the carp family is a herbivore. It is a delicacy in many Indian states. In the Kayastha community, the rohu is one of their most sacred foods and is eaten on all important occasions.

Once caught and out of the water, the color of the dolphin or dolphinfish fades to yellow. The fish's Spanish name is dorado, meaning golden maverick.

DOLPHIN (THE FISH, NOT THE MAMMAL)

"Neon" might be a better name for this fish. It is bright greenish blue over yellow sides, with irregular blue or gold blotches, and it can flash purple and chartreuse. Its head has a distinctive flat front shape. Known as dolphin or dolphinfish, this species is found in all oceans and is fond of hiding under floating debris. These fish have an eclectic diet, eating flying fish, mackerel, juvenile dolphin, crustaceans, and insects. They have also been known to eat light bulbs, plastic wrappers, rope, and string. In an effort to prevent the misconception that people are eating mammals, the dolphin or dolphinfish is now commonly known as the mahi-mahi—a fish so good they named it twice. Mahi-mahi is Hawaiian for very strong.

A beautifully colored dolphin or dolphinfish.

BASS-FISHING FALLACIES

Anglers often hamper their success by holding onto popular but incorrect assumptions about bass behaviors.

✖ **Bass prefer deep water.** In reality, bass stay near deep water just in case they require a quick escape. More often, they will be in structure that provides an easy ambush for feeding. When they do escape, it is seldom to a depth of more than 2 feet (60 cm) deeper than where they started. They prefer to stay close to a favorable temperature and level of dissolved oxygen.

✖ **Cover as much water as possible, as fast as possible.** When a jig or plastic bait hits the water, it can scare a bass. It is better to let the lure sit motionless and allow things to settle down before retrieving the lure. For how long? A couple of minutes is not too long.

✖ **The age of a bass determines its size.** Size is determined by the abundance of food, not age. Ever heard of stunted fish? Fish that can feed all the time will be bigger than fish that must rely on a smaller buffet.

✖ **Your favorite lucky lure will save the day, no matter the conditions.** The success has nothing to do with the characteristics of the lure. It is the angler's ability to experiment with retrieves and depths that make for a successful day. The experienced angler knows how to adjust his or her fishing to maximize the catch.

✖ **When in doubt, downsize the lure.** Lure selection depends on what bait is available at various times of the year. Smaller lures must also be retrieved slower than larger lures, just as smaller fish are slower than larger fish. If baitfish were faster than predatory fish, they would never be caught.

✖ **Only black or other dark-colored lures are top producers.** The bass will determine what color they prefer and they are not talking, so experiment. If you see bass following a lure but not taking, it is time to try a different color.

✖ **Some days you will not have what bass want.** Bass are opportunistic feeders and, if presented the right lure or the right color at the preferred speed, they will eat it.

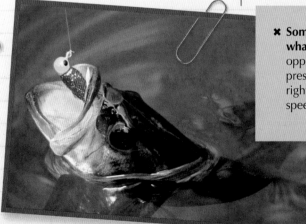

A bass will not pass up an easy meal if presented in the right way.

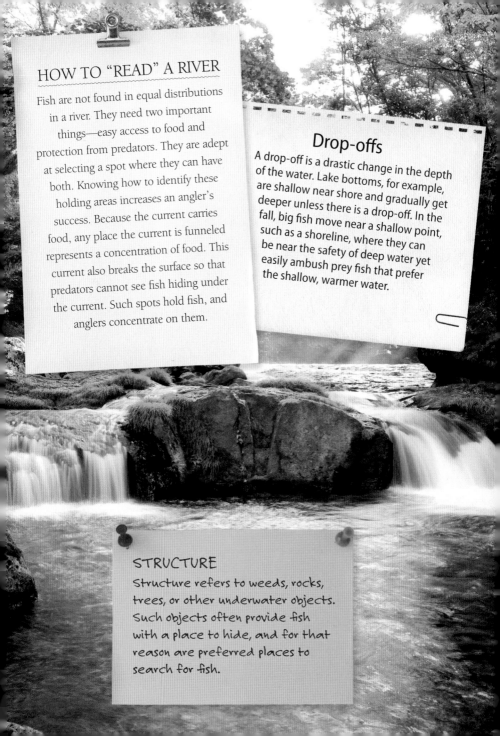

HOW TO "READ" A RIVER

Fish are not found in equal distributions in a river. They need two important things—easy access to food and protection from predators. They are adept at selecting a spot where they can have both. Knowing how to identify these holding areas increases an angler's success. Because the current carries food, any place the current is funneled represents a concentration of food. This current also breaks the surface so that predators cannot see fish hiding under the current. Such spots hold fish, and anglers concentrate on them.

Drop-offs

A drop-off is a drastic change in the depth of the water. Lake bottoms, for example, are shallow near shore and gradually get deeper unless there is a drop-off. In the fall, big fish move near a shallow point, such as a shoreline, where they can be near the safety of deep water yet easily ambush prey fish that prefer the shallow, warmer water.

STRUCTURE

Structure refers to weeds, rocks, trees, or other underwater objects. Such objects often provide fish with a place to hide, and for that reason are preferred places to search for fish.

A saltwater angler using standup tackle to land a big fish.

Standup Tackle

Standup tackle allows the angler to fight large fish.

❖ **Standup rod:** This is a short, heavy rod with a matching reel. A long rod would be a disadvantage, because it acts like a lever and would give the fish a benefit.

❖ **Rod belt/harness:** When an angler is hooked up to a heavy fish such as tuna, the strain on his or her back can be serious. A rod belt or harness made of leather or plastic provides a socket to keep the rod butt in place, and saves the angler's arms and back muscles from injury during the prolonged fight.

LANDING HEAVY FISH

✤ All modern fishing rods are tapered, with a thin tip section and a thick rear or butt section. This taper can be used to the angler's advantage.

✤ When small fish are hooked, keeping the rod tip high allows the thin tip section to act as a shock absorber, preventing light line from being broken. This is especially true for fly rods and allows 5-pound (2.3-kg) fish to be landed on 3-pound (1.4-kg) test line.

✤ When larger fish are targeted and heavier line is used, keeping the tip section high is not desired. Instead, the rod can be lowered and deliberately bent closer to the butt section. This permits much more pressure to be put on the fish so that it can be brought to hand more quickly. This is important if the fish is to be released. A fish that becomes exhausted for too long may tire beyond the point where it can be revived and released.

Big Bucks, Big Rod

FROM JAPAN, THE MUGEN SHIIPOU ISHIDAI IS A BIG ROD WITH A BIG PRICE TAG. THIS 18¾-FEET (5.7-METER) ROD IS RATED FOR 100-POUND (45-KG) LINE CLASS. A COUPLE OF THE FEATURES INCLUDE A STINGRAY SKIN GRIP AND AN 18-CARAT GOLD REEL SEAT. YOU CAN HAVE ONE FOR $10,500. WHY NOT ORDER TWO?

Archerfish

Archerfish shoot insects down out of overhanging trees with a jet of water. They are very accurate and can bring down spiders, butterflies, and grasshoppers up to 10 feet (3 meters) above the water. Immature archerfish are inaccurate and must learn the skill by practice. They could acquire the skill faster by learning from their parents but do they? No, of course they do not.

Bowfishing

Archery is a relatively obscure form of fishing, although some cultures, such as Filipino natives, have always collected their fish in this manner. A cross between hunting and fishing, bowfishing involves sighting fish and shooting them with a barbed arrow connected to the bow's reel by a cord. Carp, paddlefish, and gar are common species for bowfishing, and in the United States there is no bag limit because of their great numbers. The bowfishermen often canoe on shallow water, where the fish can be spotted, approached, and arrowed. A trophy carp may be as large as 40 pounds (18.1 kg).

Archerfish—they aim to please themselves.

Illustration from a Parisian magazine showing Peruvian natives bowfishing, 1864.

The four-eyed anableps—a spectacle without spectacles.

Oh, just pick an eye and look at it.

FOUR-EYED FISH

Anableps, a genus of four-eyed fishes, live in Mexico, Central America, and northern South America. They appear to have two sets of eyes, one above the other. The fish swims on the water's surface, searching for insects. It has adapted to this behavior by evolving so that each eye and pupil is elongated horizontally, enabling it to see both above and below the surface at the same time. The upper structure also allows it to see predators approaching from above.

Home of the Hook

+ During the Middle Ages, Redditch in England became the center of needle-making and, later, led the world in fishhook production and development.

+ The Redditch reputation supposedly began with a large monastery where the monks were skilled in the way of steel production and metal working.

+ During the mid- to late 1800s, Redditch became famous for its quality fishhooks and soon dominated the world market.

+ Partridge of Redditch, named for its founder Albert Partridge, is the only British hook maker to have survived into the 21st century, with a reputation for quality hook manufacture.

Fishing hook

Noodle Rods

These specialized long rods are very flexible and are capable of bending under little pressure, thus cushioning a light fishing line and preventing it from breaking.

Fish Fin Functions

In addition to fine alliteration, different fins serve different functions.

✤ The **tail** (or **caudal**) fin is used to propel the fish forward, and as much as 40 percent of forward movement is accomplished by the tail fin.

✤ The **dorsal** (top) and **anal** (bottom) fins prevent the fish from rolling over.

✤ The **pectoral** and **pelvic** (or **ventral**) fins are in bilateral pairs and behave as hydroplanes, controlling the depth of swimming fish. This last function also explains how fish can get a positive balance of nutrition when feeding on microscopic bugs. Moving up and down through a moving stream requires almost no energy. The fish simply tips the leading edge of its pectoral fins up and the current brings the fish to the surface. Tipping the leading edges down returns the fish to its resting place.

THOREAU

U.S.   5cents

Henry David
Thoreau

FISHY QUOTES

✦ *"The wilderness and adventure that are in fishing still recommend it to me."* Henry David Thoreau

✦ *"Every healthy boy, every right-minded man, and every uncaged woman, feels at one time or another, and maybe at all times, the impulse to go a fishin'."* Eugene McCarthy

✦ *"No angler merely watches nature in a passive way. He enters into its very existence."* John Bailey

✦ *"No human being, however great, or powerful, was ever so free as a fish."* John Ruskin

✦ *"God never did make a more calm, quiet, innocent recreation than fishing."* Izaak Walton

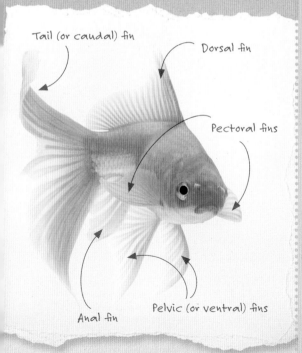

Tail (or caudal) fin

Dorsal fin

Pectoral fins

Anal fin

Pelvic (or ventral) fins

Tackling a tiny catfish.

CATFISH TACKLE

★ For smaller fish in streams, a 6- to 8-foot (1.8- to 2.4-meter) rod with 10-pound (4.5-kg) test line is recommended. Braided nylon line has almost completely been taken over by monofilament.

★ Casting or spinning reels seem to be a matter of preference. Heavy-duty reels are a necessity for heavy fish. Not only are the larger fish strong, but they are also found in places where the angler will have to horse them out using brute strength alone, and only a reel capable of withstanding the strain will do the trick.

★ The most important pieces of catfishing equipment are hooks and sinkers. Catfishermen advise to use the lightest weight possible and always use two weights. One must be a slip sinker so that the fish can pick up the bait without feeling the weight of the sinker. Should the fish feel any resistance from what should be dead bait, it will drop the bait and not get hooked. Hooks, quite simply, should be sharp. They should bite as soon as the slightest resistance is made against the hook. If not, the catfish will drop the bait and be gone.

NOODLING

Noodling is usually reserved for catfishing in the southern United States. It is a legal method in five states. Catfish prefer to hide in a hole. The noodler submerges, sticks a hand in the hole, and because catfish have no teeth, the noodler grabs the catfish by the mouth and hauls it out. Catfish can attain 60 pounds (27 kg), so the underwater grappling can be exhilarating. The noodler hopes to find a catfish, but the excitement can be almost too much to bear if it turns out to be a snapping turtle, snake, or alligator.

Getting to grips with a large catfish.

Orvis Sporting Traditions

+ Charles F. Orvis started making fly rods in the mid-1800s. He and his brother were hoteliers in the Manchester, Vermont, area. He began selling rods to his guests and his reputation grew. To take advantage of his reputation for quality tackle, he set up his own company in 1856 and started the first catalog business in the United States.

+ Orvis was not happy with the inconsistent quality of fly materials, because he wanted his customers to be confident of the superiority of what he offered. His daughter, Mary Orvis

Marbury, decided to solve the problem for dear old dad. She wrote *Favorite Flies and Their Histories* (1892). Her compilation of fly patterns and materials garnered international acclaim and was, for years, the standard desk reference for fly tyers.

+ Since its modest beginnings, the Orvis company has grown into a $200 million+ business. Each year, it donates 5 percent of its pre-tax income to various environmental conservation efforts.

FLY-TYING TOOLS

Fly tyers think that tools will make them better tyers, so they fill their benches with every kind of gadget they can find. Normally, one of each kind is not enough—the more, the better.

• Bobbin holder
• Bobbin threader
• Scissors
• Reference book
• Thread
• Thread wax
• Hair stackers
• Hackle pliers
• Hackle gauge
• Bodkin
• Whip finisher
• Dubbing twister
• Hair packer
• Vise

Fly-tyer's Vise

♦ This tool is used by fly tyers to hold a hook during the process of tying a fly. In early times, fly tyers simply held the hook in one hand and wrapped materials with the other, as depicted in *Rod-fishing in Clear Waters* (1860).

♦ As hooks became smaller, a device was required and early artisans employed a jeweler's vise because it was small, sturdy, and available.

♦ As fly tying became more popular, Ogden's Improved Fly Vise (c. 1887) was widely used. There is no written mention of the previous, presumably unimproved, version.

♦ Modern vises can cost anywhere between a few dollars to the equivalent of a month's rent. Each works nearly as well as any other, regardless of price. When tying becomes excessive, the condition is known as a tyer's vice.

FISHY QUOTES

✦ *"Fishing is the chance to wash one's soul with pure air, with the rush of a brook or with the shimmer of the sun on blue water."* Herbert Hoover

✦ *"Oh the gallant fisher's life! It is the best of any; 'Tis full of pleasure, void of strife, and 'tis beloved by many."* Izaak Walton

✦ *"It is the glory of the art of angling that its disciples never grow old. The muscles may relax and the beloved rod become a burden, but the fire of enthusiasm kindled in youth is never extinguished."* George Dawson

✦ *"Ahhh. It [saltwater fishing] is only for the strong man with a hard stomach. It is like sex after lunch."* Charles Ritz

✦ *"The fish is not so much your quarry as your partner."* Arnold Gingrich

✦ *"Nymph fishing is comparable to using a Ouija board. You're never quite sure if you're communicating with the Other World or not."* Jack Ohman

✦ *"But as for Damming, Groping, Spearing, Hanging, Twitcheling, Netting, or Firing by night, I purposely omit them, and them esteem to be used only by disorderly and rascally Fellows."* James Chetham

Spey Flies: Scottish Specialties

✴ In the 1800s, Scottish anglers on the River Spey developed a specific type of salmon fly that came to be known as the Spey fly. It was distinguished from the full-dress salmon fly by its somber body colors, long flowing hackles, and wings usually made from tented slips of bronze mallard. The earliest list of Spey flies is found in Thomas Tod Stoddart's *Angler's Companion to the Rivers and Lochs of Scotland* (1846).

✴ Unlike full-dress salmon flies, Spey flies did not retain their popularity. However, that changed in the 1970s when Pacific Northwest anglers revitalized the Spey fly for attracting Pacific salmon and steelhead. Syd Glasso led the way. His tying style is characterized by sparseness, bright colors, flowing hackles, and low-set wings. Contemporary Spey fly tyers do not shy away from violating the "rules" laid down for salmon tyers. They are constantly experimenting with new colors, materials, and methods.

Helen Elizabeth Shaw

Helen Shaw is known as the "First Lady of Fly Tying" in recognition of her skills. Born in Wisconsin in 1910, her books were intended to demystify fly tying and teach its secrets. Her books *Fly-Tying: Materials, Tools, Technique* (1963) and *Flies for Fish and Fishermen* (1989) are used by newcomers even today. She single-handedly laid bare the secrecy perpetuated by fly tyers over the centuries.

PRAISE AND CRITICISM FOR SPEY FLIES

Full-dress salmon fly purists can be a fussy lot. It is no wonder that when Spey flies were developed in the mid-1800s, some would embrace them while others would harrumph and walk away.

✗ In 1876 Francis Francis wrote, "The Spey flies are very curious productions to look at, it being customary to dress them the reverse way of the hackle, and to send the twist or tinsel the opposite way to the hackle." What can you expect from someone with the same first and last name?

✓ Alfred E. Knox, on the other hand, wrote in *Autumns on the Spey* (1872) that these drab flies were good impressions of shrimp, with the long, flowing hackles representative of legs. Since that time, the effectiveness has been proven and these flies remain popular salmon patterns not just on the River Spey.

Classic Spey fly on a background of jungle cock feathers.

Jungle Cock

THE JUNGLE COCK IS THE MALE JUNGLEFOWL NATIVE TO INDIA, SRI LANKA, SOUTHEAST ASIA, AND INDONESIA. IT IS VALUED FOR ITS "NAILS"—SOLID SPOTS OF COLOR FOUND ON ITS BREAST AND NECK FEATHERS.

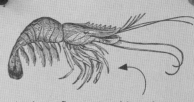

The long, flowing hackles of Spey flies imitate a shrimp's legs.

SOMETHING NEW: PATENTED FISHING LURES

There are many patented fishing lures. Some are in production, some are not, and still others, thankfully, never will be.

✤ **Illuminated fishing lures:** Built-in chemical luminescent capsules provide light.

✤ **Gold-plated lure:** Gold creates a glow and inset faceted glass stones refract light.

✤ **Ascending lure:** An upward-pointing lip causes the heavy, submerged lure to swim toward the surface, unlike buoyant lipped lures that swim downward when retrieved.

✤ **Scent-releasing lure:** A heavier-than-water lure with a cavity into which bait is inserted so that the bait is released as the lure is retrieved.

✤ **Electric lure:** An intermittent electrical output attracts fish; the output rate is adjustable by internal switches.

✤ **Sound-creating lure:** A rear section slides by means of a spring so that a clicking sound is made, both when the lure is jerked and when the rear section springs back against the forward section.

✤ **Intermittent lighted lure:** The switch contacts of a battery-operated internal light are activated when the lure is retrieved, making for intermittent flashes of light.

✤ **Lifelike frog:** The legs contain springs that extend on the retrieve and retract at rest, giving a natural-looking swimming appearance.

Alphabet Lures

This is jargon for wide-bodied, wooden crankbaits, such as the Cotton Cordell Big O and the Bomber Model A.

A realistic frog lure on a jig.

An old torpedo plug lure with a stinger hook at the tail end.

STINGER HOOK

Sometimes a fish will strike bait or lures short of the hook. This is especially true if a long bait or lure is used. A stinger hook placed near the tail end of the lure or bait increases the chance of hooking up.

Vintage National Geographic Society illustration of a northern pike pursuing a spinner lure, with a black bass and two yellow perch below.

A sailfish rounds up its prey.

What Is the Function of a Sailfish's Sail?

Sailfish feed on smaller fish that often travel in schools. The sailfish raises its sail, a highly adapted dorsal fin, and uses the sail like a curtain to round up the school into a tighter grouping called a bait ball. Concentrating the baitfish into a tighter mass improves the sailfish's feeding efficiency, because it can stun a greater number of baitfish with its bill. When sailfish hunt in packs, each takes its turn slashing into the bait ball as the others hold the baitfish in position.

WHY DO SOME FISH HAVE BILLS? *Marlin, swordfish, and sailfish have bills (don't we all?). The bill is actually an elongated upper jaw used to stun their prey. As apex predators, they often feed on large prey, and whacking them with their bill makes it easier to subdue them before swallowing.*

KITE RIG

Sailfish anglers often use a flat kite to suspend and hide their line. The flat shape of the kite causes it to fly erratically as it skips the bait on the surface like a frightened prey. This unpredictable movement excites the sailfish into striking.

Faster Than a Speeding Bullet

THE SAILFISH CAN ATTAIN SPEEDS OF 68 MILES PER HOUR (109 KPH), MAKING IT THE WORLD'S FASTEST FISH. IT SEEMS THAT EVERYTHING THIS FISH DOES IS FAST—IT BROADCASTS ITS EGGS INTO THE OCEAN AND, AFTER FERTILIZATION, THEY HATCH IN 36 HOURS.

HEAVYWEIGHT DUELERS

+ Hook a mature swordfish or marlin and the duel may last for hours. The endurance of these species comes from their long, compressed body, and their strength and speed make them a favored objective of sport fishermen.

+ To find these fish, concentrate on temperate and tropical waters of the Indian, Atlantic, and Pacific oceans. The fish spend most of their time between 600 and 2,000 feet (180 and 600 meters), but can be spotted when they are "finning"—laying on the surface.

+ These migratory fish follow cooler water in summer and warmer water in the winter. They feed on squid, mackerel, and tuna.

+ The swordfish is distinctive from other billfish in that its bill is flat in cross-section rather than round. The IGFA world record swordfish is 1,182 pounds (536.15 kg). Larger species of marlin, such as the black or Atlantic blue, can exceed 1,500 pounds (680 kg). Japan's sushi market prizes these fish highly.

Largest Fish on 1-kg Line

Guy Jacobsen from Northland, New Zealand, holds the record for the largest fish caught on a 1-kg (2.2-pound) test line with a 230-pound (104-kg) striped marlin.

Lit Up: Obvious Excitement

Pelagic fish, such as marlin, sailfish, and wahoo, "light up" with neon, powder blue colors when excited or hooked. Saltwater fly fishermen troll teaser baits and watch for the fish to light up, indicating that the angler should cast a fly to the excited fish. Doing so increases the likelihood that the fish will strike. On rare occasions, the fish will be so excited that it will jump into the boat and thrash everyone onboard.

A white marlin displaying the neon glow of excitement characteristic of this type of fish, caught on a trolling lure.

Furry and Hairy

In the good old days, Mother Nature provided everything a fly tyer could need. Natural hair is preferred by fly tyers because the normal taper makes for a gradual transition. If truth be told, almost any fur or hair can be used, but each has a unique form, length, and color that may be more suitable for a given application.

Protected Fly-tying Materials

In the United States, but not everywhere else, polar bear and baby seal fur are not allowed to be possessed, let alone used for fly tying. They were permitted years ago, and found their way into many popular fly patterns. Laws were passed to protect these animals, and possession is now verboten. The only way to possess these materials legally is to show written proof that they were collected prior to the advent of the current law. The feathers of eagles and other raptors are not allowed in possession.

SOME POPULAR FUR/HAIR

- Antelope
- Bear
- Calf
- Cat
- Coyote
- Deer
- Dog
- Elk
- Fox
- Goat
- Goose
- Hare
- Horse
- Mohair
- Moose
- Musk ox
- Muskrat
- Ostrich
- Rabbit
- Raccoon
- Sheep
- Skunk
- Squirrel
- Woodchuck
- Yak

Don't substitute my fur with bipolar bear because you'll be happy at first but sad later.

The polar bear's translucent hair makes it very desirable for fly tying, but it is now banned in some countries.

SYNTHETIC ALTERNATIVES

Once upon a time, fly-tying materials were natural. With the advent of plastics and other synthetic materials, anglers rushed to further complicate the matter of material selection. The list of synthetics grows every day, as yet another material is touted as being the latest "got-to-have-it" tying substance. Here are a few examples:

* **Antron:** This sparkle yarn is used for tying flies when a glittery sheen is desired. It can be wrapped around the shank of the hook or cut into short fibers and dubbed.

* **Chenille:** This long, thin, fuzzy material is often wound around the hook's shank to create a fly body. There are many colors and diameters. Some incorporate shiny materials to make the body sparkle and attract fish.

* **Glo Bug yarn:** This bright yarn in fluorescent colors can be spun around the hook to create bug or egg flies.

* **Tinsel:** Tinsel gives a fly sparkle. It can be used on the body, or strips can be added to wings and tails. Tinsel is made from either metal or a plastic such as Mylar. Popular plastic tinsels include Flashabou and Krystal Flash.

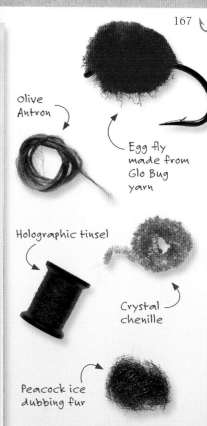

Olive Antron

Egg fly made from Glo Bug yarn

Holographic tinsel

Crystal chenille

Peacock ice dubbing fur

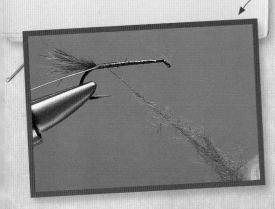

DUBBING

Fly tyers often want to cover a hook with fur or an alternative synthetic material. Dubbing involves taking small amounts of these materials and twisting them onto thread to make a yarn that is wound around the hook. Dubbing refers to both the twisting process and the material used. Both fur as well as synthetic materials can be dubbed into a yarn by this method.

Anise

Scents Make Sense for Artificial Lures

Scents (or fish attractants) for lures can be sprayed on, rubbed on as a paste or gel, or built into a plastic lure during manufacture. Is there an advantage to using them? Yes.

❶ Fish can detect minuscule concentrations of scent in water. A scented lure increases the likelihood of hooking up because it appeals to another sense used by the predator.

❷ Fish attractants can mask the scent of human oils from our hands, something that fish find unpleasant.

❸ If a fish finds a scent distasteful, it will spit the lure out quickly. An appealing scented lure will be held onto by the fish for a much longer time.

Natural Scent Flavors

SCENTS ARE OFTEN MADE BY MASHING NATURAL SPECIES OR OTHER NATURAL INGREDIENTS TO FORM A PASTE OR OIL. POPULAR SCENTS INCLUDE:

✦ ANCHOVY
✦ ANISE
✦ BLUE CRAB
✦ CORN
✦ CRAYFISH
✦ EMERALD SHINER
✦ FRESHWATER SHRIMP
✦ GARLIC OIL
✦ GIZZARD SHAD
✦ HERRING
✦ KRILL
✦ LEECH
✦ MENHADEN
✦ MINNOW
✦ MULLET
✦ NIGHT CRAWLER
✦ SALMON EGG
✦ MOLE CRAB
✦ SAND SHRIMP
✦ SARDINE
✦ SHAD
✦ SHRIMP
✦ SMELT
✦ SQUID
✦ VANILLA

Zander caught on a scented plastic worm.

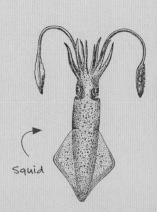

Squid

Frogfish are a type of anglerfish, named for their appearance. They are popular aquarium fish.

If a Fish Is a Fish, Can It Also Be an Angler?

Yes! Anglerfish live in deep oceans and have developed a unique response to the problem of foraging for food. Rather than swimming to case its prey, the anglerfish sits still in its camouflage and wiggles an appendage, a light-producing organ known as a photophore, in front of its open mouth. The bioluminescent appendage gives the appearance of a wiggling, wormlike creature. As a curious baitfish approaches, the anglerfish simply flares its gills and engulfs the baitfish, crushing the prey with its powerful jaws. The anglerfish is happy; the prey, not so much.

Frogfish

These bottom-dwelling anglerfish have specially adapted pectoral fins that they use to "walk" on the sea floor. They can also change color for camouflage while lying in wait for a meal to swim by.

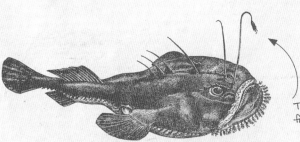

The anglerfish has its own fishing rod—a photophore.

A lithograph showing fishermen trolling for bluefish, c. 1866.

Trolling or Casting?

Virtually every lure is designed to move in some enticing way to attract the fish's interest. Lures and bait can also be manipulated to move enticingly in two basic ways—they can be trolled behind a boat and/or cast and retrieved. The advantage of trolling is the large area covered by the moving boat. Trolling is a good way to "prospect" for fish. Casting is more effective if the angler knows that the fish are holding in particular kinds of cover. For example, post-spawn largemouth bass will be found near their nests, while smallmouth bass in rivers will orient to submerged rock walls. Knowledgeable anglers concentrate their casts to such areas.

A squid-like trolling lure suitable for big-game saltwater species like marlin.

LONG POLES

These are available in lengths up to 52 feet (16 meters) and are used by match anglers. This length provides for greater accuracy and speed, because a cast is made simply by repositioning the rod rather than casting the bait. A high percentage of hook-ups can be made by fishing a short line as compared to a running line with a reel.

Record Catches (continued from page 103)

- ✦ Snook, common
  53 lb 10 oz (24.32 kg)
- ✦ Sole, lemon
  3 lb 15 oz (1.8 kg)
- ✦ Stingray, common
  444 lb 0 oz (201.39 kg)
- ✦ Sunfish, longear
  1 lb 12 oz (0.79 kg)
- ✦ Swordfish
  1,182 lb 0 oz
  (536.15 kg)
- ✦ Tarpon
  286 lb 9 oz (129.98 kg)
- ✦ Tench
  10 lb 3 oz (4.64 kg)
- ✦ Threadfin, giant African
  109 lb 5 oz (49.6 kg)

- ✦ Trevally, giant
  160 lb 7 oz (72.8 kg)
- ✦ Trout, brook
  14 lb 8 oz (6.57 kg)
- ✦ Trout, brown
  41 lb 8 oz (18.82 kg)
- ✦ Trout, cutthroat
  41 lb 0 oz (18.59 kg)
- ✦ Trout, Dolly Varden
  20 lb 14 oz (9.46 kg)
- ✦ Trout, lake
  72 lb 0 oz (32.65 kg)
- ✦ Trout, rainbow
  48 lb 0 oz (21.77 kg)
- ✦ Tuna, bluefin
  1,496 lb 0 oz
  (678.58 kg)

- ✦ Tuna, skipjack
  45 lb 4 oz (20.54 kg)
- ✦ Tuna, yellowfin
  405 lb 0 oz (183.7 kg)
- ✦ Tunny, little
  36 lb 0 oz (16.32 kg)
- ✦ Wahoo
  184 lb 0 oz (83.46 kg)
- ✦ Walleye
  25 lb 0 oz (11.34 kg)
- ✦ Whiting, European
  6 lb 13 oz (3.11 kg)
- ✦ Wrasse, ballan
  9 lb 9 oz (4.35 kg)
- ✦ Zander
  25 lb 2 oz (11.42 kg)

What's Your Class?
Record Fish by Line Strength

The International Game Fish Association (IGFA) keeps its records by line class. Generally, a record fish is determined by the line's breaking strength (known as test). A 6-pound (2.7-kg) fish caught on 2-pound (0.9-kg) test line is a record as well as a 10-pound (4.5-kg) fish of the same species caught on a 4-pound (1.8-kg) test line. Same species; both are record fish because of the breaking strength of each respective line. The all-tackle record only requires rod and reel, without regard for the breaking point of the line. So go light to get in the record book.

Casting Considerations

Different situations require the fly caster to use different casts to get the fly to the fish. Some are easy to learn; some require harsh language, adult beverages, and repeated practice.

+ **Loading a rod:** This is the process of bending a rod during the casting movement so that the weight of the fly or fly line bends the rod. When the rod's forward movement is stopped, the rod recovers from being bent and the line is thrown out, whip-like, carrying the fly with it.

+ **Back cast:** This is perhaps the most important part of a cast. In it, the line passes behind the angler before it is thrown forward, becoming the forward cast. Unless the back cast is high enough to clear the water to the caster's back, it will hit the water, the line's speed will be lost, and distance suffers.

+ **Forward cast:** This results in the line unfolding out in front of the angler, where it can be released to present the fly to the fish.

+ **Presentation:** This is the final step in casting. The goal is to land the fly in the most likely area to tempt a fish into taking it. Generally speaking, a gentle presentation is preferred because it is less likely to frighten a wary fish.

+ **False cast:** Fly casters use a false cast to mark time or dry their flies. This is done by repeating the casting stroke over and over, to and fro, without releasing the line.

+ **Double haul:** This is a technique where the angler pumps the fly line with the non-casting hand on the forward and backward elements of the cast. The pumping motion speeds the line's velocity and gives the cast additional length. Double hauling is a necessary technique for distance casting.

A fisherman using a false cast to mark time and dry the artificial fly.

The Royal Wulff fly is designed to float in a dead drift on the water's surface.

What a Drag

❋ **Drag:** Drag is a drag because it pulls the artificial fly and makes it move unnaturally on the water. Drag is the bane of fly fishermen, and many different casts have been invented to eliminate drag under various conditions.

❋ **Dead drift:** In fly casting, a dead drift is desirable because it is intended to represent the path of a helpless insect as it drifts with the current. Trout that have been fished over many times become wary of any fly that does not drift precisely without drag. A drag-free or perfect drift is the goal of fly casters, and it makes the perfect Christmas gift.

❋ **Mending a line:** This does not involve making a repair. Instead, it is a technique for improving the drift of a fly so that it appears to be a helpless insect. The mend is accomplished by throwing line (mending) upstream so that it no longer drags the fly in an unnatural manner.

CAST OFFS AND CAST ONS

Here are more types of cast than anyone could need:
- Belgian
- Bow and arrow
- Crash
- Curved
- Dapping
- Double haul
- False
- Forward
- Half-cast
- Pile
- Roll
- Side arm
- Single haul
- Steeple
- Tuck
- Underhand
- Wrist twist

BALLOONING

When the desired area cannot be reached by casting, a balloon can be attached to the line and the wind allowed to carry the line to the desired area. A jerk on the line releases the balloon and the bait drops to the target area. The balloon, hopefully, sails off to delight the child who finds it.

Dapping

This is a method of fly fishing developed in Scotland. Large artificial flies are carried by the wind as they are allowed to dance on the water, attracting fish to the surface.

A young boy proudly displays a large salmon.

ESTIMATING THE WEIGHT OF FISH

Want to brag about a large fish you have released? Not a problem. Simply apply this formula to length and girth measurements to estimate weight.

❶ Measure the girth in inches (or centimeters) and square it.

❷ Multiply this figure by the length in inches (or cm).

❸ *For inches:* Divide this value by 900 to yield the weight in pounds for thin fish such as trout, or divide by 800 for thicker fish such as bass.
For centimeters: Divide this value by 31.1 to yield the weight in kilograms for thin fish, or divide by 27.8 for thick fish.

Rather than resort to a calculator, employ the old guide's method—all trout (or thin fish) are over 6 pounds (2.7 kg); all bass (or thicker fish) are over 12 pounds (5.4 kg).

Smallest Fish Caught on a Rod and Reel

ACCORDING TO THE WORLD RECORDS ACADEMY, THIS WAS A BLACKNOSE DACE MEASURING 2.4 INCHES (6 CM) AND WEIGHING A WHOPPING 0.008 POUNDS (3.5 GRAMS).

2.4 inches (6 cm)

FISHY QUOTES

✦ *"All fishermen have the big-fish complex—we want one bigger than we have caught before, something just a little bigger than it's reasonable to hope for."* Roderick Haig-Brown

✦ *"Fish are always two inches longer, if not better than that, before they are caught. It is a very remarkable fact."* Ben Hur Lampman

✦ *"I get all the truth I need in the newspaper every morning, and every chance I get I go fishing, or swap stories with fishermen, to get the taste of it out of my mouth."* Ed Zern

✦ *"There is in every fisherman… a peculiar tendency toward exaggeration which he can recognize in his companion, but is rarely capable of seeing it in himself!"* Zane Grey

✦ *"A fish is larger for being lost."* Japanese proverb

✦ *"Anglers exaggerate grossly and make gentle and inoffensive creatures sound like wounded buffalo and man-eating tigers."* Roderick Haig-Brown

✦ *"Some of the best fishing is done not in the water, but in print."* Sparse Grey Hackle

✦ *"Do not tell fish stories where the people know you; but particularly, don't tell them where they know the fish."* Mark Twain

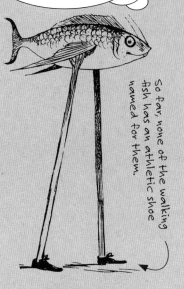

I want to be an actor. If I get a walk-on part, it could be my big break.

So far, none of the walking fish has an athletic shoe named for them.

TAKE A HIKE

While all fish swim, some can also leave the water and walk. Examples include the mudskipper, walking perch, and northern snakehead. They use various means of perambulation, and most can spend significant lengths of time out of the water. Some literally use a swimming motion to move across the ground; some use their pectoral (front) fins as if they were legs and pull themselves forward; others use a combination.

SOME NOTABLE CATFISH

✤ **Largest catfish:** The Mekong giant catfish is the largest freshwater fish in the world. It can grow up to 10 feet (3 meters) long and weigh 650 pounds (295 kg). As large as it is, the Mekong giant's numbers have been reduced by 95 percent by overfishing. It is now on the brink of extinction. Some experts think there may only be a few hundred Mekong giants left.

✤ **Kitty-sized catfish:** The smallest variety of catfish is the toothpick fish (candirú) of the Amazon River, the only vertebrate parasite thought to attack humans. This 6-inch (15-cm) species is known for an alleged tendency to invade and parasitize the human urethra. However, very few cases have been verified, and some discredited as myth. You can make up your own mind and take your own chances.

The Panaque genus of catfish is notable for being the only fish able to eat and digest wood.

✤ **Stinging catfish:** Some catfish can sting, with painful results. The stinger is a hollow ray on the dorsal or pectoral fins. The poison is created in the tissue at the base of the ray. Some catfish are simply nuisance stingers, while others create more damage. The *Heteropneustes* of South Asia is an air-breathing fish. Its sting is serious enough to send the unfortunate to hospital. On an even more serious note, the sting of the *Plotosus lineatus* can cause death. This is one of the few true marine catfish and it lives in the Pacific near India.

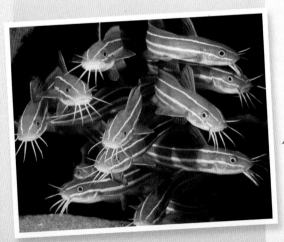

The striped eel catfish, Plotosus lineatus, has highly venomous spines on the dorsal and pectoral fins.

The glass catfish is a popular ornamental aquarium fish. Its body is transparent, and the bony structure looks like an x-ray.

Some catfish species, such as the gafftopsail catfish, can communicate. They do this by rubbing fins against their swim bladder, causing vibrations.

GAFFTOPSAIL CATFISH

Iridescent Shark Catfish

THE IRIDESCENT SHARK IS REALLY A CATFISH, AND IS NAMED BECAUSE OF THE IRIDESCENT GLOW OF JUVENILES AND ITS SHARK-LIKE APPEARANCE. IT IS A COMMON FOOD FISH IN PARTS OF ASIA.

Insect Life Cycles

Fly tyers imitate the developmental stages of insects to match the form being fed upon by the fish.

Adult mayfly

+ **Nymphs:** This is the juvenile stage of insects such as mayflies and stoneflies. The crawling nymph lives underwater and is covered by a hard exoskeleton. The term nymph is used to describe any artificial fly that imitates the underwater stage of insects and invetebrates.

+ **Larvae:** This is the underwater stage of insects such as caddis and midges. They usually have soft bodies and progress through a pupal stage before adulthood.

+ **Emergers:** Insects passing through the nymphal or pupal form and in the process of rising to the surface just before they hatch into winged adults are called emergers. Emergers float helplessly in the current, trapped in the surface film, and represent an easy meal for feeding fish. Fly fishermen cast imitations of this stage in front of the fish in order to tempt the fish to strike. Some of the simplest emergers are nothing more than a fur body and simple wing.

Some Important Insects

❖ **Mayflies** are the most beautiful and delicate of aquatic insects. Their wings stand up like the sails on a boat.

❖ **Caddis flies** (or sedges) look like small moths, with tent-like wings that lay flat over the body when the fly is at rest.

❖ **Stoneflies** are large, awkward insects and easy fare for fish.

❖ **Chironomid** (or midges) are especially important because their high-density hatches attract fish.

❖ **Terrestrials** are non-aquatic insects that find their way onto the water and are eaten by fish.

Mayfly emergers

FISHING THE SPINNER FALL

The last act of insects such as the mayfly is to mate and lay eggs on the water. These spinners do this by repeatedly rising and falling above the river, depositing eggs each time they drop low until all of the eggs are gone. Then the spinner falls, dying on the surface. Fish gorge on this easy feast, and anglers make imitations of spinners because of this. Angling at this time is called fishing the spinner fall.

HOW TO TIE A SIMPLE FLY

Although it may seem like magic, tying a fly is a simple affair. The techniques below are used for even the most complex patterns. This example is an F Fly, a simple but deadly little fly. It can be tied in a variety of body colors to suggest anything from a small mayfly to a caddis fly or even a stonefly. A small black version is effective when there are little dark-colored terrestrials on the water.

The F Fly is easy to tie in even the smallest sizes.

❶ Tighten a hook in the vise so that it is grasped at the bend of the hook.

❷ Wrap thread in close wraps along the shank of the hook from the eye to a point opposite the barb. This layer of wrapped thread prevents materials from slipping around on the hook shank.

❸ Catch in four pheasant tail fibers by taking several wraps of thread around the end of the fibers.

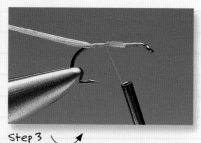

Step 3

❹ Wrap the thread back to the eye.

❺ Wrap the feather fibers around the hook, starting where it is tied to the hook and working up to just behind the eye.

❻ Secure the end of the feather fibers with several wraps of thread. Trim off the excess feather fibers.

Step 5

❼ Position two small cul de canard feathers along the top of the shank and tie with three firm wraps of thread behind the eye.

❽ Trim off the excess feather at the eye, then wrap several turns of thread over the end of the feathers.

❾ Finish the fly by making several overhand knots near the hook eye. Trim the thread and you are done.

Step 9

PISCATORIAL PREVARICATION

Anglers do not lie. They may stretch the truth, obfuscate, or otherwise deliberately confuse each other, but they absolutely, hardly ever lie. The following are offered as proof. Your money back is not guaranteed.

What the angler said	*What the angler meant*
"I caught them on a size 24 midge."	"I missed them on a size 6 streamer."
"I've been a fly fisherman for 50 years."	"I've fished 50 times in the past 50 years."
"I took a dozen last night."	"They all came from the same can of sardines."
"I can cast 90 feet of fly line."	"It takes me three casts to do it, each being 30 feet."
"My wife says I can go fishing any time I want."	"I was divorced eight years ago."

Life Span

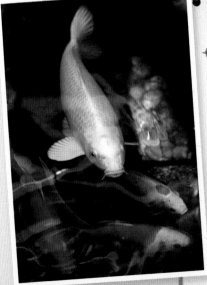

Ornamental koi ↰

+ **Longest:** Hanako, a Japanese koi fish, died on July 7th, 1977, at age 226. Koi fish are prized as ornamentals, and are passed from generation to generation. Hanako's age was confirmed following an examination of its scales at the Laboratory of Domestic Science at Nagoya Women's College in Japan.

+ **Shortest:** The 3/8- to 3/4-inch (1- to 2-cm) pygmy goby lives, for 59 days, on the Great Barrier Reef. Female pygmy gobies lay 400 eggs that are guarded by the male. For three weeks, the larvae live in the open ocean. They then return to the reef for about ten days and mate. The pygmy goby snatched the title of shortest life span away from the African turquoise killifish, which lives for 12 weeks in seasonal rain pools.

Angling Art Form

From the mid-1800s, Japanese anglers have used the art form of gyotaku ("gyo," meaning fish; "taku," rubbing) to record their catch. The imprint of the fish is made by coating one side with sumi ink and pressing paper against the fish. Each print made in this manner is unique, and many Japanese participate in this art form. What better reason could there be to rub a fish?

Anglers have used the camera to prove their piscatorial prowess since the early days of photography. Here, two proud fishermen shake hands over a catch of perch and walleye in front of a painted backdrop in a photographer's studio in Minnesota, 1913— ideal proof that they were not stretching the truth (this time).

AN ABRIDGED HISTORY OF BASS FISHING:
A TACKLE-DRIVEN DEVELOPMENT

1760: Naturalist William Bartram observes Indians in the American South catching largemouth bass.

1881: Dr. James Henshall writes *Book of the Black Bass* and pronounces the smallmouth bass "inch for inch and pound for pound, the gamest fish that swims."

1897: William Shakespeare, Jr. patents a level-wind device for bait-casting reels, making them easier to use by reducing the chance of backlash.

1902: James Heddon receives his patent for a floating wooden lure carved from a barrel bung, or plug.

1910: The Creek Chub Bait Co. offers the Creek Chub Wiggler, the first plug with a metal diving lip to make the lure wiggle when retrieved.

1915: The William J. Jamison Co. produces the Shannon Twin Spinner, a gaudy lure with two blades attached to a wire weed guard—the precursor of spinnerbaits.

1920: Finding no natural frogs to use as bait, Alan P. Jones and Urban Schreiner carve pork back fat and invent the first pork frogs. Two years later, they form the Uncle Josh Bait Co.

1932: President Franklin D. Roosevelt creates the Tennessee Valley Authority. The thousands of lakes created are stocked with bass and interest in bass fishing goes swimmingly.

1937: DuPont files a patent for nylon and later creates nylon monofilament line.

1938: Spinning reels are introduced in the United States and, when combined with nylon monofilament, make cast-and-retrieve fishing easier for all anglers.

1948: Skeeter builds a new category of fishing craft designed for bass fishing.

1949: Inexpensive fiberglass rods are introduced and replace expensive bamboo.

1949: Nick and Cosma Creme of Akron, Ohio, pour melted plastic into molds and create the first soft plastic worm—the Creme Wiggle Worm.

1950: The Dingell-Johnson Fish Restoration Act is passed, placing excise taxes on fishing equipment.

1954: The Zero Hour Bomb Co. (now Zebco) makes the first closed-face spin-casting reel and casting becomes foolproof for novices.

1955: Outdoor writer Earl Golding hosts first organized bass tournament, the Texas State Bass Tournament.

1957: Carl Lowrance introduces the first portable sonar units that can detect both the bottom and fish.

1968: Ray Scott organizes 100 members into the Bass Anglers Sportsman Society (B.A.S.S.).

1971: Starting with $10,000 borrowed money, John Morris starts Bass Pro Shops.

1972: Fenwick and Shakespeare introduce graphite fishing rods, which quickly replace fiberglass.

1972: Ray Scott starts the "Don't Kill Your Catch" program as part of B.A.S.S.

1973: Don Butler patents first live wells for bass boats.

1984: The Wallop-Breaux amendment passes. To date, this legislation has put more than $3 billion into state fisheries programs.

1992: Larry Nixon becomes the first professional angler to earn over $1 million.

2000: According to B.A.S.S., 30 million people fish for bass, spending $50 to $70 billion annually.

"Lure" ice sculpture from the World Ice Art Championships held in Fairbanks, Alaska.

Index

Credits

Quarto would like to thank and acknowledge the following for supplying photographs and illustrations reproduced in this book. All other images are the copyright of Quarto Publishing plc. While every effort has been made to credit contributors, Quarto would like to apologize should there have been any omissions or errors—and would be pleased to make the appropriate correction for future editions of the book.

Key: *a* above; *b* below; *l* left; *r* right; *c* center

Corbis: Bettmann 51, 96; Christopher Rennie/Robert Harding World Imagery 75; Geoffrey Clements 131; National Geographic Society 163; Minnesota Historical Society 181a

istockphoto: tacojim 26al; inhauscreative 27a

Miscellaneous: Tony Lolli 67b; NASA 118b; Frederick Dally/Library and Archives Canada/C-065097 129cr; Brian.gratwicke 138a

National Oceanic and Atmospheric Administration/ Department of Commerce: 85ar; 113; Allen Shimada 151b

Rex Features: CSU Archives/Everett Collection 101

Shutterstock: Lukiyanova Natalia/frenta 1a; Dewitt 1b, 88al, 152; ILLYCH 2; hunta 3, 55b; novvy 10–11; frantisekhojdysz 12al; Pborowka 12cr; Alterfalter 12 (sardines); Morphart 13al, 56a, 58a; Slava Gerj 13b; Lineartestpilot 14a, 109b, 119b; bernd.neeser 14b; photobank.kiev.ua 15a; Francesco Abrignani 15b; Kharidehal Abhirama Ashwin 16a; IgorGolovniov 16b, 175b; Rich Carey 17a; stephan kerkhofs 17b, 176b; joppo 18 (maggots); Anneka 19al; basel101658 19r, 67a; 3d_kot 19bl; Elena Pal 20l; Scott Richardson 20r; FAUP 21a; patrimonio designs limited 21b, 53c; Helen & Vlad Filatov 22 (fertilizer background); Sportstock 23a; Sergey Goruppa 24al, 134b, 142b, 150; Dabjola 24 (top and bottom maggots); Henrik Larsson 24 (center maggot), 141a (maggot); Kevin H Knuth 24br; zebra0209 25a; abracadabra 27b; Mark Herreid 28a, 148ac; Bruce MacQueen 28b; Lilyana Vynogradova 29a (fish background); Klara Viskova 29ac (man holding fish); Commons 29b, 141b; Steven Russell Smith Photos 30b; Alaskan Guide 31; Andi Berger 32b; A New Focus 33a; Nagib 33b; Wire_man 34a; Bubica 34b; Krzysztof Odziomek 35a; p|s 35b; Michael-John Wolfe 36a; Schalke fotografie | Melissa Schalke 37; Holbox 38a, 99b, 112b, 146b, 154, 165; Stephen Bures 38b; Mashe 39a; HUANG, CHI-FENG 39c; JonMilnes 39b; rook76 40a, 110c, 111a; Natursports 40b; Michael Rothschild 41a; BW Folsom 41cl; W. Scott 41b; FimkaJane 42a; Petr Malyshev 42b, 64a; Kuma 43c (felt); Ljupco Smokovski 43r; Peter Zachar 46; LeCajun 47a; Fedor Kondratenko 47b; Krasowit 48l, 114a, 148ar, 162a, 170b; David Brimm 48ar, 66ac, 149ar; Optimarc 48br; Bobb Klissourski 49a; TerryM 49b; Dewald Kirsten 52; Jason Vandehey 53ar; ChipPix 54a, 120; John Kropewnicki 55a;

Michael Vigliotti 56c; oksana.perkins 56b; chantal de bruijne 57a; Richard Griffin 57b; Adquarters 58b; Nancy A Thiele 59a; walter71 60; withGod 61a; EML 61b; Mikael Goransson 62a; Steffen Foerster Photography 62b; Panamsky 63b; Rob kemp 64b; Grintan 65b; Imageman 66al, 140; Nito 66ar; Timothy R. Nichols 66b; diado hari 68; Niar 69a; BEPictured 70 (feather background); Tovkach Oleg 71 (feather background); Victoria Goncharenko 71br; Aliaksei Lasevich 72a; Dhoxax 72b; Stocksnapper 73c; EcoPrint 73b; David Dohnal 76; Tramper 77; Ammit 80a; Jpegwiz 80b; Daria 81a; George Muresan 81bl; Hintau Aliaksei 81br; Mountainpix 83a; Aleksandrs Marinicevs 84; Brandelet 85al; walter71 86ar; Ancher 86bl, 110a; Ivan Sazykin 86br; Zheltyshev 87a, 148al; AlessandroZocc 87cl; Ignite Lab 87bl; Geoff Hardy 87br; Dennis Cox 88bl; sahua d 88br; Stephen Mcsweeny 89a; Stephen Bonk 89b; Subbotina Anna 90a; Julia Ivantsova 90b; Rob Hainer 91a; Forbis 91b; Tish1 92al; Pedro Nogueira 92ar; Antonio Abrignani 92b, 155b; Andrew Ferguson 93; Tund 94l; Ben Haslam/Haslam Photography 94r; Andreas Gradin 95a; Racheal Grazias 95b; RAFal FABRYKIEWICZ 98bl; Tribalium 98br; Jumpingsack 99a; CataVic 100a; Feliks Kogan 100b; HelleM 102a; Carmen Steiner 102b; Dewitt 104l; Noedelhap 104r; Guentermanaus 105a; Newnolik 105b; Ryan Carter 106a; Sean Gladwell 106bl; Ivan Montero Martinez 106br; Texturis 107ar; Loren Rodgers 107br; Dietmar Hoepfl 107bl; Vilmos Varga 108; Kiev.Victor 112a; Undersea Discoveries 115b; Dec Hogan 117a, 144b; Maxim Tupikov 118a; Steve Brigman 119a, 127b; Crystal Kirk 121; 8464181369 122a; Ugorenkov Aleksandr 122bl; hartphotography 122br; Christy Liem 123al; Urosr 123ar; Stacey Lynn Payne 123b; Sandra Cunningham 126a; Anton Novik 126b; Gpeet 128a; Ryhor M Zasinets 130l; Eric Isselée 130r, 181b; meirion Matthias 133; Mikeledray 135a; aquariagirl1970 135b; Suto Norbert Zsolt 136; Arend 137a; R Perreault 137b; Michaeljung 138b; Eldred Lim 139a; Bluehand 139c; Farferros 139b; Richard Peterson 141a (catapult); Artiomp 142a; Photobank 143ar; James Steidl 143b; MrHanson 144a; ori-artiste 145a; Karolina L 145b; Daniel Petrescu 146a; Sergey Mikhaylov 147a; SeDmi 147c; Shebeko 147b; Brasiliao 148b; Okicoki 149b; Dr Ajay Kumar Singh 151a; Albert Barr 151c; SoulAD 153; Johannes Kornelius 155a; Gallimaufry 156a; Zelfit 156b; tristan tan 157a; Tischenko Irina 157b; David Ryznar 158b; Boris15 160; Roman Krochuk 161a; Stephanie Frey 162b; Catmando 164a; NitroCephal 166a; Andrey Yurlov 166b; vsevolod izotov 168bl; bierchen 169a; Iralu 171; Jack Z Young 172; Zooropa 173b; Keith Publicover 174a; iliuta goean 176a; Kristina Stasiuliene 177a; Miroslav K 177b; Awei 178a; Attila JANDI 178b; Joy Brown 180b; Gary Whitton 183. Various background papers: emily2k; Feng Yu; Javarman; Lars Lindblad; Marilyn Volan; Nils Z; Nuttakit; Optimarc; Petrov Stanislav Eduardovich; Picsfive; Ragnarock; Robyn Mackenzie; silver-john; suradech sribuanoy; Valentin Agapov; valzan

U.S. Fish and Wildlife Service: Duane Raver 111b, 127a; Timothy Knepp 124; F. Eugene Hester 125; Robert W. Hines 134a; Glenn Young 149al

U.S. Geological Survey: Noel Burkhead/Howard Jelks 26b